EASY ENTERTAINING

EASY ENTERTAINING

Delicious and simple recipes
for warming autumn suppers and fabulous party food

ATLANTIC WORLD

For best results when cooking the recipes in this book, buy fresh ingredients and follow the instructions carefully. Make sure that everything is properly cooked through before serving, particularly any meat and shellfish, and note that as a general rule vulnerable groups such as the very young, elderly people, pregnant women, convalescents and anyone suffering from an illness should avoid dishes that contain raw or lightly cooked eggs.

Standard spoon measurements are level and are based on the following:1 tsp = 5 ml, 1 tbsp = 15 ml

The electric oven temperatures in this book are given for conventional ovens with top and bottom heat. When using a fan oven, the temperature should be decreased by about 20–40ºF / 10–20ºC – check the oven manufacturer's instruction book for further guidance. The cooking times given should be used as an approximate guideline only.

Although the recipes in this book are believed to be accurate and true at the time of going to press, neither the authors nor the publisher can accept any legal responsibility or liability for any errors or omissions that may be made nor for any inaccuracies nor for any harm or injury that may come about from following instructions or advice given in this book.

CONTENTS

SEASONAL SOUPS

PUMPKIN SOUP WITH SAGE AND BACON

Prep and cook time: 45 min Serves 4

2 tbsp butter

1 onion, finely chopped

1 clove garlic, finely chopped

150g floury potatoes, diced

500g pumpkin flesh, diced

650 ml vegetable stock

100 ml single cream

10g ginger, grated

½ tsp lemon juice

Salt and ground black pepper

1 pinch grated nutmeg

100g bacon, diced

25g butter

5 sage leaves

1 tbsp extra virgin olive oil

1 Heat the butter in a pan and fry the onion and garlic until softened. Add the potatoes and pumpkin and cook for a few minutes.

2 Stir in the vegetable stock and cook for 25 minutes until the vegetables are soft.

3 Transfer the soup in batches to a blender or food processor and blend until smooth. Return to the pan and add the cream, ginger, lemon juice, salt, pepper and nutmeg.

4 Fry the bacon in a small pan in the butter until crisp. Remove and drain on kitchen paper. Add the sage to the pan and fry for 30 seconds.

5 Add the bacon and sage to the soup, drizzle with the olive oil and season with ground black pepper.

CREAM OF POTATO SOUP WITH CRISPY BACON

Prep and cook time: 45 min   Serves 4

25g butter

1 large onion, chopped

500 g floury potatoes, peeled and cut into small pieces

1 litre vegetable stock

salt and pepper

1 bay leaf

4–5 tbsp double cream

To garnish:

1–2 tbsp snipped fresh chives

4 rashers crisply grilled streaky bacon

1   Heat the butter in a large pan and add the onion. Cook slowly over a low heat for about 5 minutes until softened.

2   Add the potatoes, stock, bay leaf and a sprinkling of salt and pepper and bring to a boil. Simmer for 20–25 minutes, skimming off any froth, until the potatoes are tender. Cool slightly and remove the bay leaf.

3   Transfer the soup in batches to a blender or food processor and blend until smooth. Return to the pan and stir in the cream. Season to taste with salt and pepper.

4   Reheat gently, but do not boil. Pour into serving bowls, sprinkle over the chives and crumble the bacon on top.

PARSNIP SOUP

Prep and cook time: 45 min   Serves 4

2 tbsp cumin seeds

3 tbsp vegetable oil

1 onion, chopped

1 clove garlic, chopped

750g parsnips, chopped

750 ml vegetable stock or water

Salt and pepper

125 ml single cream

Cayenne pepper

1   Toast the cumin seeds in a dry pan for 30 seconds and set aside.

2   Heat the oil in a large pan and gently cook the onion and garlic until soft. Stir in the cumin seeds, reserving a few for the garnish, and cook for 2 minutes.

3   Add the parsnips to the pan, stir well then add the stock or water. Bring to a boil then simmer gently for 20–25 minutes or until the parsnips are tender.

4   Transfer the soup in batches to a blender or food processor and blend until smooth. Return to the pan and season to taste with salt and pepper.

5   Pour into serving bowls, stir in the cream and garnish with the reserved cumin seeds and a sprinkle of cayenne pepper.

ROOT VEGETABLE SOUP WITH GARLIC TOAST

Prep and cook time: 1 hour   Serves 4

For the soup:

3 tbsp olive oil

1 onion, diced

1 large leek, sliced

4 garlic cloves, finely chopped

800g assorted root vegetables, roughly chopped

1 litre vegetable stock

2 tbsp chopped flat-leaf parsley

For the toasted garlic bread:

1 bulb garlic

2 tbsp olive oil

1 French loaf, sliced and toasted

1   Heat the oil in a large pan and gently cook the onion, leek, garlic and root vegetables for about 5 minutes, until softened.

2   Add the stock and bring to a boil. Reduce the heat, cover and simmer for 40 minutes, until the vegetables are tender, skimming frequently to remove surface scums.

3   For the garlic toast, heat the oven to 200°C / 400°F / Gas Mark 6. Drizzle the bulb of garlic with the olive oil.

4   Wrap the garlic in foil and roast for about 20 minutes until golden brown. Squeeze the soft roasted garlic out onto the toasted bread.

5   Pour the soup into serving bowls, garnish with the parsley and serve with garlic toast.

MUSHROOM SOUP

Prep and cook time: 40 min   Serves 4

55g butter

1 onion, chopped

2 cloves garlic, finely chopped

500g mushrooms, chopped

2 tbsp flour

Salt and pepper

900 ml vegetable stock

200 ml dry white wine (or stock)

75 ml dry sherry

Flat-leaf parsley, to garnish

1   Heat the butter in a large pan, add the onion and garlic and cook gently until soft, but not browned.

2   Add the mushrooms and and sprinkle with the flour. Cook until soft and season with salt and pepper to taste.

3   Stir in the stock and wine and bring to a boil. Cover and simmer for 10 minutes. Stir in the sherry and serve immediately garnished with parsley.

SWEET POTATO SOUP WITH GINGER

Prep and cook time: 45 min   Serves 4

3 tbsp oil

2 onions, chopped

5-cm piece ginger, finely chopped

1 clove garlic, finely chopped

4 sweet potatoes, peeled and chopped

1.1 litres vegetable stock

200 ml crème fraîche

Salt and freshly milled black pepper

Grated nutmeg

1   Heat the oil in a large pan and cook the onions until they are starting to soften.

2   Add the ginger and garlic and cook for a further 2–3 minutes.

3   Add the sweet potatoes and cook for a further 10 minutes, stirring occasionally.

4   Stir in the stock, cover and simmer very gently for about 20 minutes, until the sweet potato is tender. Cool slightly.

5   Transfer the soup in batches to a blender or food processor and blend until smooth.

6   Return to the pan and add the crème fraîche. Season to taste with salt, pepper and nutmeg. Reheat gently and serve garnished with nutmeg.

CARROT AND ORANGE SOUP

Prep and cook time: 30 min   Serves 4

2 tbsp butter

1 onion, chopped

6 carrots, peeled and grated

1 baking potato, peeled and grated

600 ml vegetable stock

2 oranges, grated zest and juice

2 tbsp crème fraîche

Pinch cayenne pepper

2 tbsp fresh parsley, chopped

Salt and freshly milled pepper

1   Sauté the chopped onion in hot butter, add the grated carrots and potato, season with salt, cover and cook for about 5 minutes.

2   Now pour in enough vegetable stock so that the vegetables are covered. Add the orange zest, cover and simmer for a further 10 minutes.

3   Purée the soup until smooth. Add the orange juice and the crème fraîche and stir. Pour in a little additional vegetable stock if needed, depending on the thickness of the soup.

4   Season to taste with salt and cayenne pepper. Garnish with chopped parsley and freshly milled pepper and serve.

SIMPLE STARTERS

PAPRIKA CHICKEN WITH ONIONS

Prep and cook time: 20 min   Serves 4

6 tbsp olive oil

1 onion, finely diced

1 garlic clove, chopped

1 tsp paprika

2 chicken breasts, skinned and cut into bite-size pieces

1 tbsp balsamic vinegar

Fresh coriander sprigs, to garnish

1   Heat the oil in a pan and gently fry the onion until translucent. Add the garlic and paprika and cook for 1 more minute.

2   Turn up the heat, add the chicken pieces and cook for about 6 minutes, stirring frequently, until the chicken is browned and cooked through.

3   Add the balsamic vinegar, stir and cook for a further 2–3 minutes. Serve immediately, with fresh coriander to garnish.

SPICY KING PRAWNS

Prep and cook time: 20 min   Serves 4–6

1 tbsp vegetable oil

3-cm piece fresh ginger, peeled and grated

2 garlic cloves, minced

2 spring onions, trimmed and chopped

450g raw large prawns, peeled and deveined

1 tbsp tomato purée

2 tsp chilli bean sauce

1 tsp cider vinegar

1 tsp sugar

2 tsp sesame oil

Fresh coriander leaves, to garnish

1   Heat the oil in a large frying pan or wok. Add the ginger, garlic and spring onions and stir-fry for 20 seconds.

2   Add the prawns and stir-fry for 1 minute.

3   Add the tomato purée, chilli bean sauce, cider vinegar, sugar and sesame oil and stir-fry for another few minutes. Serve at once, garnished with coriander.

TARRAGON MUSHROOMS

Prep and cook time: 10 min   Serves 4

4 tbsp butter

250g button mushrooms

1 garlic clove, finely chopped

½ bunch tarragon, chopped

100 ml white wine

4 tbsp crème fraîche

4 slices baguette

Salt and freshly ground pepper

tarragon leaves, to garnish

1   Heat the butter in a pan and cook the mushrooms for about 1 minute, or until golden brown.

2   Add the garlic and chopped tarragon, toss briefly and stir in the white wine. Boil until reduced, then stir in the crème fraîche and cook for about 1 minute.

3   Toast the baguette slices on both sides.

4   Season the mushrooms to taste with salt and pepper and place on the toasted baguette slices. Serve garnished with tarragon.

MUSHROOM BRUSCHETTAS

Prep and cook time: 25 min   Serves 4

4 tbsp olive oil

1 small onion, finely chopped

1 garlic clove, crushed

200g button mushrooms, finely chopped

50g black olives, pitted and finely chopped

12 slices baguette, toasted

Salt and freshly ground pepper

2 tbsp parsley, finely chopped, to garnish

1   Heat 3 tbsp of oil in a pan and gently fry the onion until soft.

2   Add the garlic, cook for 1 minute then add the mushrooms and cook for 10 minutes. Stir in the olives and season with salt and pepper.

3   Brush the toasted bread with the remaining oil, spoon over the mushroom mixture and garnish with the chopped parsley.

GRILLED POLENTA SLICES WITH MUSHROOMS

Prep and cook time: 25 min plus 30 min standing time   Serves 4

For the polenta:

500 ml vegetable stock

125g instant polenta

Salt and ground black pepper

Grated nutmeg

For the mushroom medley:

3 tbsp oil

1 onion, diced

1 clove garlic, finely chopped

400g mixed mushrooms, e. g. chanterelles, porcini and oyster mushrooms, chopped if necessary

1 tbsp chopped parsley

1 tbsp chopped basil

Salt and ground black pepper

Basil, to garnish

1   Grease a 25cm round baking tin with oil.

2   Place the stock in a pan and bring to a boil. Gradually stir in the polenta, bring to a boil again and allow the polenta to absorb the stock for around 5 minutes. Remove from the heat and season with salt, pepper and nutmeg. Spread the polenta in the baking tin and leave to cool for at least 30 minutes.

3   Heat 2 tablespoons oil in a frying pan and fry the onion and garlic until softened. Add the mushrooms and fry for a few minutes stirring continuously. On a medium heat, allow the liquid to evaporate. Add the herbs and season with a little salt and pepper.

4   Turn the polenta out of the baking tin and cut into 8 slices.

5   Heat the remaining oil in a ridged frying pan and fry the polenta pieces on both sides until browned.

6   Place on warmed serving plates with the mushrooms and garnish with basil.

CARPACCIO OF BEEF

Prep and cook time: 20 min plus 20 min chilling   Serves 4

450g beef tenderloin

1 tbsp creamed horseradish

Juice of 1 lemon

2 tbsp olive oil

Rock salt

Freshly crushed black pepper

50g Parmesan cheese, shaved

1 handful rocket

1   Wrap the beef in cling film and place in the freezer for 20 minutes.

2   Slice the beef with a very sharp knife as thinly as possible and lay the slices on a serving platter or 4 individual plates.

3   Dot the creamed horseradish over the beef, drizzle over the lemon juice and oil and sprinkle with salt and pepper.

4   Scatter over the Parmesan cheese and rocket and serve immediately.

ROASTED PUMPKIN AND GORGONZOLA SALAD

Prep and cook time: 50 min   Serves 4

1 medium pumpkin, peeled and seeds removed

150 ml olive oil

2 tbsp balsamic vinegar

200g baby spinach or salad leaves

325g Gorgonzola, crumbled

Salt and freshly ground pepper

1   Heat the oven to 200°C / 400°F / Gas Mark 6.

2   Cut the pumpkin into slim wedges and cut each in half. Brush with a little of the oil and place on a baking tray. Bake for 20–30 minutes or until tender. Remove from the oven and let cool.

3   Mix the remaining oil with the balsamic vinegar, season with salt and pepper and set aside.

4   Arrange the salad leaves on serving plates, add the cooked pumpkin and Gorgonzola, and drizzle over the balsamic dressing.

ONIONS STUFFED WITH GOAT'S CHEESE

Prep and cook time: 45 min plus 8 hours to marinate Serves 4

300g goat's cheese, chopped

4 slices prosciutto, chopped

1 tbsp red peppercorns, crushed

1 tsp black peppercorns, crushed

4 bay leaves

4 garlic cloves, chopped

Zest and juice of 2 lemons

500 ml extra virgin olive oil

4 medium red onions

250 ml chicken stock

Thyme sprigs, to garnish

1 Place the goat's cheese in a bowl with the prosciutto, crushed peppercorns, bay leaves, garlic and lemon zest. Cover with the oil and lemon juice and refrigerate for 8 hours or overnight.

2 Heat the oven to 230°C / 450°F / Gas Mark 8.

3 Peel the onions, cut off the tops and hollow out. Place the onions and their tops in a baking dish. Add the stock to the bottom of the dish, cover with foil and bake for 20 minutes until the onions are just soft. Remove from pan with a slotted spoon and set aside.

4 Preheat the grill to a high heat. Remove the goat's cheese from the refrigerator. Strain the liquid from the goat's cheese; keep the spices, prosciutto and garlic, and discard the bay leaves.

5 Stuff the hollowed onions with the cheese/prosciutto mixture and place in a shallow baking dish or pan. Cook under the grill for 3 minutes or until the tops are golden brown. Garnish with thyme and serve.

CHEESE SOUFFLÉS

Prep and cook time: 40 min Serves 4

100g butter, softened

50g fresh breadcrumbs

5 eggs, separated

150g cheese, Emmental or Gruyere, grated

4 tbsp double cream

2 tbsp crème fraîche

2 tbsp flour

½ tsp paprika

Pinch nutmeg

Salt and freshly ground pepper

1 Grease 4 individual ramekins or ovenproof tea cups with a little of the butter and sprinkle the breadcrumbs over the buttered surfaces.

2 Heat the oven to 200°C / 400°F / Gas Mark 6.

3 Beat the egg yolks and remaining butter together with the cheese, cream, crème fraîche, flour, paprika and nutmeg. Season with salt and pepper.

4 Whisk the egg whites until they form stiff peaks and fold into the egg yolk and cheese mixture.

5 Spoon into the ramekins and bake for 10–15 minutes or until golden brown and well risen.

MINI SAVOURY TARTS

Prep and cook time: 20 min   Makes 12

200g sun-dried tomatoes in oil

400g thawed frozen puff pastry

3 mini mozzarella balls, thinly sliced

1 small aubergine, thinly sliced

Salt and freshly ground pepper, to taste

4 tbsp pine nuts, toasted

Olive oil, as needed

1 handful rocket leaves, trimmed, to garnish

1   Preheat the oven to 200°C / 400°F / Gas Mark 6. Line a baking sheet with foil or parchment.

2   Finely chop the tomatoes, adding a little of the tomato oil, until they resemble a paste.

3   Roll out the puff pastry and cut out 12 circles using an 8-cm round cookie cutter. Spoon some of the tomato mixture on the top and season with salt and pepper. Top with a few slices of mozzarella, followed by aubergine slices. Sprinkle with a few pine nuts and drizzle lightly with olive oil.

4   Place tarts on the baking sheet and bake until lightly browned, about 15 minutes. Garnish with the rocket leaves and serve immediately.

SCALLOPS WITH PROSCIUTTO

Prep and cook time: 30 min   Serves 4

6 tbsp olive oil

2 courgettes, sliced

6 large scallops, sliced in half horizontally

4 slices prosciutto, chopped into strips

50g shaved Parmesan cheese

Lemon wedges, to serve

For the herb oil:

Large handful mixed fresh herbs e.g. parsley, basil, thyme

125 ml olive oil

Juice of 1 lemon

Salt and freshly ground pepper

1   First make the herb oil: place the herbs in a blender with the oil and lemon juice and whiz until smooth. Season with salt and pepper and set aside.

2   Heat 3 tbsp of oil in a frying pan and gently fry the courgettes until tender. Remove from the pan and set aside.

3   Heat the remaining oil in the frying pan and cook the scallops for 2 minutes on each side or until browned.

4   Lay the courgettes in serving dishes and drizzle with the herb oil. Add the scallops, prosciutto and Parmesan cheese, and serve with lemon wedges.

WARMING SUPPERS

CHICKEN WITH SWEET POTATOES AND CRANBERRIES

Prep and cook time: 1 hour 50 min   Serves 4

1 tbsp oil

1.5 kg corn fed chicken

1 red onion, sliced

1 garlic clove, chopped

5 sweet potatoes, peeled and cut into quarters

225g cranberries

1 litre hot chicken stock

Salt and pepper

Sprigs fresh rosemary

1 Heat the oil in a frying pan and fry the chicken, breast side down, for about 10 minutes until browned. Put the chicken in a casserole dish.

2 Fry the onion and garlic in the pan until softened then put them into the dish with the chicken. Add the sweet potatoes and cranberries to the pan.

3 Season the stock with salt and pepper to taste and pour over the chicken. The chicken and vegetables should be covered with liquid. Tuck in the sprigs of rosemary.

4 Cover and cook for about 1-1½ hours until the chicken is thoroughly cooked and the vegetables are tender.

Comfort Food

CHORIZO STEW WITH CRÈME FRAÎCHE

Prep and cook time: 50 min   Serves 4

250–300g chorizo

500g pack of soup vegetables (including, for example, carrot, leek, celery, parsnip, turnip)

3 tbsp olive oil

2 onions, sliced

1–2 cloves garlic, chopped

400g potatoes, peeled and cubed

400g tin of tomatoes

500–800 ml vegetable stock

Salt and pepper to taste

1 bay leaf

1–2 tsp dried oregano

200g tin of chickpeas

Small tub of crème fraîche

Fresh parsley

1   Peel the chorizo sausage and cut into slices.

2   Chop the soup vegetables into bite-size pieces.

3   Fry the chorizo sausage in a little oil, then add the onions and the garlic and sauté until soft.

4   Add the potatoes, soup vegetables, tomatoes and pour in the vegetable stock. Season with salt and pepper to taste and add the bay leaf and oregano.

5   Cover with a lid and simmer gently for about 30 minutes on a low heat.

6   Drain the chickpeas, then add to the stew and heat. Season with more salt and pepper if necessary and serve with a spoonful of crème fraîche and a sprinkling of fresh parsley.

RATATOUILLE WITH CHICKEN

Prep and cook time: 1 hour 15 min   Serves 4

1 whole chicken (about 1.25kg), jointed or 4 chicken pieces

Salt and pepper

Olive oil, for frying

2 red onions, cut into wedges

1 aubergine, thickly sliced

2 courgettes, thickly sliced

1 red pepper, sliced

2 cloves garlic, chopped in half

1 tsp tomato purée

200 ml chicken stock

4 tomatoes, stems removed

1 tsp paprika

Fresh basil leaves, to garnish

1   Heat the oven to 180°C / 350°F / Gas Mark 4.

2   Season the chicken pieces with salt and pepper and fry in hot oil in a flameproof casserole until golden brown. Remove and set aside.

3   Fry the onion, aubergine and courgette. Sauté the pepper and the garlic, then add the tomato purée and pour in the chicken stock. Add the tomatoes and paprika and more salt and pepper to taste.

4   Put the chicken pieces on top, skin side up, and place the casserole in the oven for 30–40 minutes. Spoon a little stock over the chicken from time to time and stir.

5   Adjust the seasoning with salt and pepper if necessary, sprinkle some basil leaves over the top and serve.

TANDOORI FISH MASALA

Prep and cook time: 40 min plus 2 hours to marinate
Serves 4

4 fish fillets (sea bream, cod) about 200g each

Salt

2 tbsp lemon juice

2 tbsp ghee or clarified butter, melted

For the marinade:

400g yoghurt

3 tbsp vinegar

1 large onion, finely chopped

3–5 garlic cloves, crushed

½ tsp freshly grated ginger

½–1 tsp turmeric

1 pinch each of salt, ground coriander, garam masala, chilli powder

Pepper, according to taste

1 tbsp spring onion rings, 1 tbsp lime zest and ½ red chilli, deseeded and cut into rings, to garnish

1   Rub the fish fillets with salt and drizzle lemon juice over the top. Place the fish in a baking dish, greased with ghee or clarified butter.

2   For the marinade, mix all the ingredients together with 1–2 tablespoons water. Pour over the fish and place in the refrigerator for 2 hours. Turn the fish from time to time.

3   Pre-heat the oven to 180°C / 350°F/ Gas Mark 4. Put the fish in the oven and cook for about 15–20 minutes. Add a little water if needed. Before serving, place the fish under a pre-heated grill for a few minutes to brown (according to taste).

4   Divide between 4 bowls, placing a fish fillet in the centre of each bowl. Scatter a few chilli and spring onion rings over the fish and sprinkle some lime zest on the top. Serve hot.

CHICKEN MOLE

Prep and cook time: 45 min Serves 4

1 tbsp oil	1 tsp ground cinnamon
4 boneless chicken thighs	Pinch ground cloves
4 chicken drumsticks	2 tbsp plain flour
1 onion, chopped	2 x 400g cans chopped tomatoes
3 garlic cloves	
2 sticks celery, chopped	450 ml chicken stock
1 red pepper, deseeded and sliced	50g dark chocolate (70% cocoa solids), chopped
1 tsp chilli powder	Salt and pepper
1 tsp ground cumin	

1   Heat the oil in a frying pan and fry the chicken pieces until browned on all sides. Remove from the pan and set aside.

2   Add the onion, garlic, celery and red pepper to the pan and fry for 5 minutes.

3   Add the spices and flour to the pan and cook for 2 minutes.

4   Stir in the tomatoes and stock, then add the chocolate. Season to taste with salt and pepper. Bring to a boil.

5   Add the chicken to the sauce in the pan. Cover and simmer for about 25 minutes, until the chicken is tender.

Warm and Spicy

CHICKEN AND CHICKPEA CURRY

Prep and cook time: 1 hour Serves 4

1 tbsp oil

8 boneless, skinless chicken thighs, each cut into 4 pieces

25g butter

2 onions, finely chopped

4 garlic cloves, crushed

1 red chilli, sliced and seeds discarded

1 tsp ground cumin

3 tsp cardamom seeds, crushed

1 tsp ground tumeric

2 tsp garam masala

1 tsp grated ginger

1 tsp salt

2 bay leaves, crushed

300 ml chicken stock

1 x 400g can chickpeas

Coriander, to garnish

1 Preheat the oven to 200°C / 400°F / Gas Mark 6.

2 Heat the oil in a frying pan and cook the chicken pieces until browned. Remove from the pan.

3 Add the butter to the pan and when hot add the onions, garlic and chilli. Cook until just beginning to colour.

4 Add the spices and salt. Cook for 1 minute. Add the bay leaves and stock and bring to the boil. Stir in the chickpeas.

5 Place the chicken in a baking dish and pour over the onion mixture. Cook in the oven for about 30 minutes until the stew is bubbling and the chicken is thoroughly cooked.

6 Serve garnished with coriander leaves.

LAMB STEW WITH DUMPLINGS

Prep and cook time: 1 hour 20 min   Serves 4

600g lamb, for braising, cubed

2 tbsp sunflower oil

2 onions, sliced

2 cloves garlic

600 ml beef stock

Salt and freshly milled pepper

2 stalks celery

200g potatoes, cubed

200g sweet potatoes, peeled and cubed

2 carrots, chopped

2 bay leaves

For the dumplings:

200g plain flour

1 egg

1 tbsp thyme leaves, dried

100 ml milk

Grated nutmeg

1   Fry the meat in hot oil until browned on all sides. Add the onions and the garlic and pour in the stock. Season and bring to a boil then simmer for about 30 minutes.

2   Add all the vegetables and bay leaves and simmer for a further 45 minutes.

3   In the meantime make the dumplings. Mix the flour, egg and thyme and add enough milk to form a dough.

4   Season with salt and freshly grated nutmeg. Use a teaspoon to form tiny balls, then place in boiling, salted water and simmer for about 10 minutes.

5   Season the stew with salt and pepper and serve with a few dumplings.

BAKED COD WITH POTATOES, OLIVES AND TOMATOES

Prep and cook time: 45 min Serves 4

700g new potatoes

1 onion, chopped

150 ml vegetable stock

700g cod fillets

450g cherry tomatoes

100g black pitted olives

Juice of 1 lemon

2 tbsp olive oil

1 tbsp chopped fresh parsley leaves

Salt and freshly ground pepper

1 Preheat the oven to 180°C / 350°F / Gas Mark 4.

2 Thoroughly wash and slice the potatoes. Place in a heat-resistant baking dish with the chopped onion.

3 Pour the vegetable stock over the top. Season with salt and pepper. Bake in the oven for about 15 minutes.

4 Cut the fish into large pieces.

5 Remove the dish from the oven, add the tomatoes, fish and olives and season with salt and pepper. Drizzle with the lemon juice and olive oil.

6 Continue cooking for another 15 minutes (add a little water if necessary). Garnish with parsley and serve.

CREAMY CHICKEN WITH LEEKS

Prep and cook time: 35 min Serves 4

2 tbsp olive oil

1 onion, chopped

4 baby leeks, shredded

4 boneless chicken breasts, skinned and cut into thick slices

Salt and pepper

1 tbsp plain flour

300 ml chicken stock

200 ml crème fraîche

2 tbsp chopped fresh tarragon

Lime wedges, to garnish

1   Heat the oil in a large frying pan and add the onion and leeks. Cook gently for 2 minutes, then remove 1 tbsp of the lightly cooked leeks and set aside to garnish.

2   Add the chicken to the pan, season generously with salt and pepper and cook for 5 minutes until browned on all sides.

3   Sprinkle over the flour and cook for 1 minute, then gradually stir in the stock. Cover the pan and simmer for 15 minutes.

4   Stir the crème fraîche and tarragon into the chicken and heat through for 2–3 minutes. Check that the chicken is thoroughly cooked through. Serve the chicken with rice and garnish with the reserved leeks and a lime wedge.

CHICKEN AND CASHEW STIR-FRY

Prep and cook time: 30 min   Serves 4

4 tbsp sesame oil

4 chicken breasts, skinned and cut into chunks

2 tbsp cornflour

1 green chilli pepper, deseeded and chopped

1 green pepper, deseeded and chopped

3 spring onions, sliced

8 water chestnuts (tinned), sliced

75g cashew nuts

4 tbsp oyster sauce

Juice of 1 lime

2–3 tbsp light soy sauce

1   Heat the oil in a wok or deep frying pan until smoking. Dust the chicken pieces with the cornflour and stir-fry them for 3–4 minutes or until slightly crispy. Remove the chicken from the wok.

2   Add a little more oil to the wok and fry the chilli pepper for 1 minute. Add the green pepper and spring onions and cook for 2 more minutes.

3   Return the chicken to the wok with the water chestnuts and cashew nuts. Stir in the oyster sauce, lime juice and soy sauce and serve immediately with rice.

ROASTED SALMON FILLETS WITH PEPPERS

Prep and cook time: 50 min   Serves 4

4 pieces salmon fillet

Juice of 1 lemon

1 garlic clove

1 red pepper, deseeded and cut into strips

1 yellow pepper, deseeded and cut into strips

1 green pepper, deseeded and cut into strips

1 onion, halved and sliced

100 ml vegetable or fish stock or white wine

4 tbsp olive oil

1 tbsp fennel seeds

Salt and freshly ground pepper

Basil leaves, to garnish

1   Heat the oven to 200°C / 400°F / Gas Mark 6.

2   Brush the fish with 2 tbsp lemon juice and leave to stand for 10 minutes.

3   Halve the clove of garlic and rub the cut side over the inside of an ovenproof dish.

4   Season the peppers and onion with salt and pepper and place in the roasting dish. Pour over the stock and drizzle with 2 tbsp oil.

5   Season the fish fillets with salt and pepper and lay on top of the peppers. Sprinkle with the fennel seeds, drizzle over the rest of the oil and lemon juice and cover with foil.

6   Bake for 20–30 minutes or until the fish is cooked through. Serve scattered with basil leaves.

Impress without stress

COQ AU VIN

Prep and cook time: 1 hour Serves 4

4 tbsp plain flour

Salt and pepper

1 chicken, cut into 4 pieces

150g butter

225g shallots

1 garlic clove, crushed

120g thickly sliced bacon, diced

225g chestnut mushrooms

1 bottle dry white wine

3 sprigs fresh thyme plus some for garnish

For the beurre manié

25g butter

25g plain flour

1 Preheat the oven to 180°C / 350°F / Gas Mark 4.

2 Put the flour into a large shallow dish and season generously with salt and pepper. Dip the chicken portions in the flour to coat.

3 Melt the butter in a large flameproof casserole dish. When foaming, add the chicken portions and fry until browned all over, turning as needed.

4 Add the shallots, garlic and diced bacon and fry until golden brown. Stir in the mushrooms. Pour in the wine and add the thyme. Bring to the boil then cover the casserole.

5 Cook in the oven for 40 minutes until the chicken and vegetables are tender.

6 Put the butter and flour for the beurre manié in a small bowl and mix together. Return the coq au vin to the heat and cook over a medium heat, stirring in the beurre manié, a small piece at a time, until the sauce thickens slightly and is glossy. Serve garnished with fresh thyme.

BEEF GOULASH

Prep and cook time: 1 hour 45 min Serves 4

1kg chuck beef, cubed

3 tbsp oil

4 onions, sliced

2 cloves garlic, chopped

1 tbsp sweet paprika

½ tsp ground caraway seeds

500 ml beef stock

Salt and freshly milled pepper

1 bay leaf

1 tsp hot paprika

1 tbsp fresh marjoram leaves, to garnish

1   Heat the oil in a frying pan. Fry the beef on all sides, a few pieces at a time, until browned.

2   Reduce the heat and sauté the onions together with the meat.

4   Add the sweet paprika and the ground caraway seeds, then pour in the beef stock. Add the bay leaf, garlic and hot paprika.

5   Simmer over a low heat for about 1–1½ hours, stirring occasionally. Add a little water if necessary.

6   When cooked, season to taste with salt and pepper and sprinkle a few marjoram leaves over the top. Serve with bread or boiled potatoes.

SPICY PORK RAGOUT

Prep and cook time: 2 hours 15 min Serves 4

800g pork neck, cut into bite-size cubes

4 tbsp olive oil

1 large onion, finely sliced

3 cloves garlic, finely chopped

1 stick celery, finely chopped

1 carrot, peeled and sliced

500g canned tomatoes

200 ml red wine

1 tbsp tomato purée

2 tsp sugar

Salt & freshly milled pepper

200 ml vegetable stock

½ tsp cayenne pepper

1 tsp paprika

Fresh oregano, to garnish (optional)

1   Heat 4 tablespoons of olive oil in a stew pot and quickly brown the meat on all sides. Take out and set aside.

2   Then in the same oil, sweat the onion, celery, carrot and garlic over a medium heat Add the meat, sweat briefly with the vegetables, then pour in the red wine.

3   Cook until the wine has evaporated slightly, then stir in the tomatoes and tomato purée. Season with salt and pepper and add the sugar.

4   Bring to a boil, then add the vegetable stock and simmer over a low heat for about 2 hours. If the ragout becomes too dry while cooking, stir in 1–2 tbsp of water.

5   15 minutes before the end of cooking time, stir in the cayenne pepper and paprika. Check the seasoning and add a little more salt and pepper to taste. Garnish with the oregano before serving.

CHICKEN CAPONATA

Prep and cook time: 1 hour 10 min   Serves 4

4 chicken legs

8 sage leaves

2 garlic cloves, chopped

2 red chilli peppers, deseeded
and chopped

4 tbsp olive oil

2 tbsp lemon juice

For the caponata:

4 tomatoes

2 tbsp olive oil

1 medium aubergine, coarsely chopped

1 yellow pepper, sliced

1 onion, sliced

1 celery stalk, sliced (leaves reserved for garnish)

50g pitted black olives

1 tbsp capers

White wine vinegar

Salt and freshly ground pepper

1   Preheat the oven to 180°C / 350°F / Gas Mark 4.

2   Take the chicken legs and separate the drumstick from the thigh at the joint. Put one sage leaf under the skin of each piece of chicken.

3   Mix together the garlic, chilli pepper, olive oil and lemon juice. Rub into the chicken and put in a roasting pan.

4   Bake the chicken in the preheated oven for about 40 minutes until golden brown.

5   Blanch the tomatoes, immerse in cold water and remove the skins. Slice into quarters and remove the seeds.

6   Sauté the aubergine in hot oil until lightly browned.

7   Add the pepper, onion and sliced celery. Season with salt and pepper. Cook, covered, for about 10 minutes, stirring occasionally.

8   Add the tomatoes, olives and capers. Cook, uncovered, for about 4 minutes more. Season to taste with the vinegar, salt and pepper.

9   Divide the vegetables among the plates and arrange the chicken pieces on top. Garnish with the reserved celery leaves and serve.

POTATO SOUFFLÉS

Prep and cook time: 1 hour 10 min Serves 4

575g potatoes

Butter, for greasing

225g filo pastry

1 onion, peeled and finely chopped

50g butter

100g quark

4 sprigs fresh marjoram, leaves stripped and finely chopped

75g grated hard cheese

2 eggs, separated

Nutmeg

Salt and freshly ground pepper

Marjoram, to garnish

1 Preheat the oven to 180°C / 375°F / Gas Mark 5.

2 Cook the potatoes in salted boiling water for 30 minutes until soft. Drain, peel and press through a ricer. Leave to steam dry and cool slightly.

3 Grease 4 ramekins with butter.

4 Lay out the filo pastry in double layers and cut out squares about 15×15 cm. Line the ramekins with the pastry and brush with melted butter.

5 Fry the onion in hot butter until translucent and let cool slightly.

6 Mix the quark with the chopped marjoram, two thirds of the hard cheese, the egg yolks, onion and potatoes.

7 Beat the egg whites until stiff, then fold carefully into the potato mixture and season to taste with salt, pepper and nutmeg.

8 Spoon into the ramekins and scatter with the remaining cheese.

9 Bake for about 25 minutes in the middle of the preheated oven until golden brown. Garnish with marjoram sprigs and serve.

ROASTED PUMPKIN AND FENNEL

Prep and cook time: 35 min   Serves 4

4 tbsp olive oil

1 medium pumpkin or butternut squash, peeled, deseeded and diced

2 bulbs fennel

175g chopped dates

Salt and freshly ground pepper

1   Heat the oven to 180°C / 350°F / Gas Mark 4.

2   Heat the oil in a large frying pan and gently fry the pumpkin or squash for 2 minutes.

3   Chop the green tops of the fennel and set aside. Chop the fennel flesh and add to the pumpkin/squash. Stir well and transfer to a roasting pan. Pour over 250 ml water and roast in the oven for 15 minutes.

4   Stir the fennel tops and dates into the vegetables, season with salt and pepper and return to the oven for 10 minutes or until the vegetables are golden brown.

ROASTED VEGETABLES WITH APPLES

Prep and cook time: 50 min Serves 4

6 tbsp olive oil

4 small red onions, outer skins removed

4 medium new potatoes, scrubbed and cut into wedges

4 sprigs thyme

Salt and freshly ground pepper

4 small dessert apples

300g cherry tomatoes, on the vine

1 tbsp balsamic vinegar

1   Heat the oven to 180°C / 350°F/ Gas Mark 4.

2   Heat the oil in a roasting pan and add the onions and potatoes, coat with the hot oil and add the thyme sprigs. Sprinkle with salt and pepper and put into the oven to roast for 20 minutes.

3   Add the apples and tomatoes to the pan, baste everything with the cooking juices and return to the oven for 20 minutes.

4   Drizzle over the balsamic vinegar, transfer to a warmed serving dish and serve immediately.

BALSAMIC APPLES AND RED ONIONS

Prep and cook time: 35 min Serves 4

4 tbsp olive oil

2 red onions, cut into wedges

2 large cooking apples, peeled, cored and cut into quarters

Salt and freshly ground pepper

2 tbsp balsamic vinegar

1   Heat the oven to 200°C / 400°F / Gas Mark 6.

2   Heat the oil in a roasting pan and add the onions. Cook for 2 minutes then add the apples and stir so everything is coated with oil.

3   Season with salt and pepper, cover with kitchen foil and roast in the oven for 10 minutes.

4   Remove from the oven and discard the foil. Sprinkle the balsamic vinegar over the onions and apples, baste well and return to the oven for 10 more minutes.

STUFFED PEPPERS

Prep and cook time: 50 min   Serves 4

3 tbsp olive oil

150g cooked rice

100g cherry tomatoes, halved

1 carrot, peeled and coarsely grated

100g feta cheese, crumbled

2 tbsp freshly chopped basil

4 red peppers, halved lengthwise and deseeded

About 100g white bread crumbs

Salt and freshly ground pepper

1   Preheat the oven to 180°C / 350°F / Gas Mark 4.

2   Grease a baking dish with 1 tbsp of oil.

3   Place the rice in a large bowl. Mix in the tomatoes, carrot, crumbled feta and basil and season with salt and pepper.

4   Spoon the filling into the pepper halves and place in the baking dish. Scatter with bread crumbs, drizzle with the remaining oil and bake in the preheated oven for 30 minutes until golden brown.

Bonfire Bites

GRILLED CHICKEN WITH MANGO DIP

Prep and cook time: 45 min plus marinating time 12 h   Serves 4

For the chicken:

16 chicken wings

Few dashes Tabasco sauce

4 tbsp oil

1 tbsp honey

1 tbsp ketchup

2 tbsp chilli sauce

1 tbsp vinegar

Salt and freshly milled pepper

1 spring onion, finely chopped

For the mango dip:

1 mango

1 tbsp honey

1 tbsp rosemary leaves

Lime juice, to taste

1   For the marinade, mix the Tabasco sauce, oil, honey, ketchup, chilli sauce and vinegar. Season well with salt and pepper and stir in the spring onions.

2   Brush the chicken pieces with the marinade. Cover and marinate, preferably overnight. Then cook on a grill over a medium heat for 15–20 minutes, turning frequently.

3   For the mango dip, finely purée the flesh of a mango with 1 tablespoon honey and 1 tablespoon rosemary leaves. Add a little lime juice to taste.

4   Serve the chicken wings with a dish of mango dip.

BAKED POTATOES
WITH CHEESE AND BACON TOPPING

Prep and cook time: 45 min   Makes 20

For the potatoes:

10 medium-sized baking potatoes

2 tbsp olive oil

Salt and freshly ground pepper

20 slices bacon

20 slices cheese

1 handful lamb's lettuce, to garnish

For the chive cheese dip:

250g cream cheese

400 ml sour cream

½ tsp vegetable stock granules

2–4 tbsp fresh chives, chopped

Salt and ground white pepper

1   Pre-heat the oven to 200°C / 400°F / Gas Mark 6.

2   Scrub the potatoes and then cut in half lengthways. Brush a roasting pan with olive oil and place the potatoes on the roasting pan, cut side downwards. Bake in the oven for about 25 minutes.

3   In the meantime, mix together all ingredients for the chive cheese dip, reserving 1 tablespoon of chopped chives for the garnish. Season to taste with salt and pepper, then spoon into a bowl and garnish with chives.

4   When the potatoes are cooked, remove from the oven. Heat the grill to 250°C / 475°F.

5   Carefully take the potatoes off the roasting pan and season the flat side with salt and pepper. Place the bacon on the top of the potato and cover with cheese. Place under the grill until golden brown. Serve the potatoes on a plate, together with the cheese dip. Garnish with a few leaves of lamb's lettuce.

BEANS WITH PORK

Prep and cook time: 4 hours plus 12 hours soaking time   Serves 8

450g haricot beans, rinsed and soaked overnight
1 tbsp oil
400g belly pork, cut into 5 cm cubes
1 onion, finely chopped
1 garlic clove, crushed
110 ml molasses
2 tsp wholegrain mustard

1 tbsp tomato purée
1 tbsp Worcester sauce
100 ml white wine vinegar
125 ml water
1 tsp cayenne pepper
Pinch salt

1   Heat the oven to 140 °C / 275°F / Gas Mark 1.

2   Put the soaked beans and enough cold water to cover them into a large pan and bring to a boil. Boil briskly for 10 minutes. Drain and set aside.

3   Heat the oil in a frying pan and fry the pork until golden brown. Remove and set aside.

4   Add the onions and garlic to the pan and cook for 5 minutes until softened.

5   Combine all the ingredients except the salt, until well mixed. Transfer the mixture to a greased casserole or baking dish. Cover and cook for 3–4 hours, until the beans are tender. Add salt to taste.

SPARE RIBS

Prep and cook time: 1 hour plus 2 hours to marinate   Serves 4

1½ kg spare ribs
2 tbsp soft brown sugar
1 tbsp soy sauce
2 tsp mustard powder
2 garlic cloves, crushed
2 tbsp tomato ketchup

1 tbsp Worcestershire sauce
2 tbsp red wine vinegar
1 tsp salt
1 tsp black pepper

1   Mix together all the ingredients apart from the ribs to make a marinade. Coat the ribs and leave to marinate for at least 2 hours, turning from time to time.

2   Heat the oven to 180°C / 350°F / Gas Mark 4.

3   Place the ribs in a roasting tin, pour over the marinade so they are all well coated and roast for about 45 minutes, basting frequently, until the ribs are tender.

CHILLI BEEF WITH WINTER VEGETABLES

Prep and cook time: 1 hour 20 min   Serves 6

5 tomatoes

Oil, for frying

600g beef, for stewing (such as from the leg, cut into cubes)

2 onions, chopped

2 cloves garlic, chopped

Pinch of curry powder

Cayenne pepper

Ground cumin

400 ml beef stock

600g baking potatoes, peeled and diced

200g tin of chickpeas, washed and drained

200g frozen peas

2 tbsp pumpkin seeds

Salt and pepper

1 Drop the tomatoes into boiling water for a few seconds, refresh in cold water, then skin, quarter, deseed and dice.

3 Heat the oil and brown the meat on all sides. Add the onions and garlic and fry briefly, then add the curry powder, cayenne pepper and cumin. Add the stock, cover and stew for about 30 minutes.

4 Add the potatoes, tomatoes, chickpeas and peas and simmer gently for a further 40–50 minutes. Stir occasionally and add more stock if necessary.

5 Toast the pumpkin seeds in a dry frying pan. Season the casserole to taste and serve scattered with pumpkin seeds.

DESSERT

BAKED APPLES WITH NUT FILLING

Prep and cook time: 1 hour Serves 4

4 large apples, cored

75g light brown sugar

3 tbsp water

1 lemon, finely grated zest

110g sultanas

55g chopped almonds

Icing sugar

Bay leaves, to decorate

1 Heat the oven to 180°C / 350°F / Gas Mark 4.

2 Mark a line with a sharp knife around the centre of each apple, through the skin, but not through the flesh. Place the apples in a baking dish.

3 Spoon the sugar into the cavities of the apples. Put the water into the baking dish and bake for about 30 minutes until almost tender.

4 Mix together the lemon zest, sultanas and almonds and divide between the apples, pressing the mixture into the cavities.

5 Cook for a further 15 minutes until the apples are soft and cooked through. Serve hot with the juices poured over. Sift a little icing sugar over the apples and decorate with bay leaves.

POACHED RED WINE PEARS

Prep and cook time: 30 min plus 3 hours chilling time Serves 4

1 unwaxed lemon

150g sugar

1 cinnamon stick

750 ml red wine

4 small-medium cooking pears

8 walnut halves

1 Slice the lemon and put in a saucepan with the sugar, cinnamon stick and red wine. Bring to a boil then simmer gently for about 10 minutes.

2 Peel the pears, leaving the stalks on. Remove the cinnamon stick and lemon slices from the red wine. Stand the pears upright in a deep saucepan and pour in the wine, making sure that it covers the pears. Cover the pan and poach the pears over a low heat for about 10 minutes.

3 Take the pears out of the poaching liquid and stand on individual serving plates.

4 Boil the red wine until reduced to a syrupy consistency. Add the walnuts and mix into the sauce. Pour the hot red wine sauce over the pears and leave until cold before serving.

RASPBERRY-PLUM CRUMBLE

Prep and cook time: 40 min Serves 4

For the filling:

6 dark red plums, quartered, stones removed
and washed

200g raspberries

75g caster sugar

For the crumble:

125g plain flour

100g butter, cut into pieces

100g light brown sugar

To garnish:

1 tbsp coarse sugar

1 Heat the oven to 180°C / 350°F/ Gas Mark 4.

2 Put the plums, raspberries and caster sugar into a saucepan with 1 tbsp water. Simmer for 5 minutes to soften the fruit.

3 Meanwhile, put the flour and butter into a food processor and whiz until the mixture forms crumbs, or put into a bowl and rub the mixture together with your fingertips. Add the brown sugar and pulse to combine.

4 Spoon the fruit into a shallow medium baking dish. Spoon the crumble mixture on top, sprinkle with coarse sugar and bake for 20 minutes or until pale golden.

PANNA COTTA

Prep and cook time: 15 min plus at least 5 hours chilling time   Serves 4

1 vanilla bean

500 ml whipping cream

50g sugar

3 leaves white gelatine

½ tsp lemon zest

225g raspberries

1   Slice the vanilla bean in half lengthwise. Scrape out the seeds.

2   Cook the cream with the sugar, vanilla seeds and pod over low heat for about 3 minutes.

3   Soften the gelatine in a dish with cold water.

4   Remove the vanilla bean from the cream. Remove the pan from the heat.

5   Squeeze out the gelatine and add it to the vanilla cream. Stir to dissolve. Add the lemon zest.

6   Rinse out 4 moulds with cold water. Fill with the cream and refrigerate for at least 5 hours.

7   Turn the panna cotta out of the moulds (to dislodge: briefly dip the moulds in hot water). Decorate with the raspberries and serve.

CHOCOLATE SOUFFLÉ

Prep and cook time: 1 hour 15 min Serves 4

Butter, for greasing

100g sugar, plus extra for sprinkling

175g dark chocolate, at least 65% cocoa solids

5 tbsp milk

2 tsp cocoa powder

5 eggs

2 tsp plain flour

icing sugar, for dusting

1   Preheat the oven to 180°C / 350°F / Gas Mark 4.

2   Put a deep baking tin, half-filled with water, on the lowest shelf of the oven. Grease a soufflé dish with butter and sprinkle with sugar. Place in the refrigerator.

2   Break up the chocolate. Put the milk, cocoa powder and half of the sugar in a saucepan and heat until warm. Remove from the heat, add the chocolate and stir until melted.

3   Separate the eggs. Stir the egg yolks and the flour into the chocolate mixture. Whisk the egg whites and the remaining sugar together until stiff. Fold carefully into the chocolate mixture.

4   Turn the mixture into the prepared soufflé dish and place in the oven in the baking pan. Bake for about 50 minutes. The middle of the soufflé should be soft and runny. Dust with icing sugar and serve immediately.

CRÊPES SUZETTE

Prep and cook time: 45 min plus 20 min standing time   Serves 4

For the crêpes:

2 eggs

250 ml milk

125g plain flour

1 tbsp sugar

Butter, for frying

For the sauce:

4 unwaxed oranges

4 tbsp sugar

40g butter

5 tbsp Grand Marnier

1   To make the pancakes, beat the eggs, milk, flour and sugar to a smooth batter and leave to stand for 20 minutes.

2   To make the sauce, cut thin strands of zest from 2 of the oranges. Peel all the oranges using a sharp knife, removing all the white pith and skin. Cut down between the segments and remove the segments, catching the juice into a bowl as you work. Squeeze any remaining juice out of the oranges into the bowl.

3   Heat the sugar and butter in a frying pan until caramelized. Stir in the orange juice. Simmer until a smooth sauce is formed, and then add the orange zest and segments. Remove from the heat.

4   Heat a little butter in another frying pan and make 8 thin crêpes, one after the other. Fold each into a triangle. Place the crêpes in the orange sauce and warm briefly.

5   Add the Grand Marnier and flambé. Serve on warmed plates with the orange sauce.

CARAMELISED CHOCOLATE CREAM

Prep and cook time: 45 min plus 4 hours chilling
Serves 4

425 ml double cream

50g dark chocolate, broken into pieces

3 fresh egg yolks

80g caster sugar

1 Heat the oven to 150°C / 300°F / Gas Mark 2. Grease 4 ramekins.

2 Heat the cream in a pan and bring to a boil.

3 Remove from the heat and add the chocolate, stirring until melted. Allow to cool slightly.

4 Mix together the egg yolks and half the sugar.

5 Whisk in the cream and chocolate mixture until blended. Pour into the ramekins.

6 Place the ramekins in a roasting tin and half fill with hot water. Place a piece of foil loosely over the tin. Cook for 25–30 minutes until firm around the edges but still slightly wobbly in the centre. Allow to cool.

7 Chill for at least 4 hours.

8 Heat the grill until very hot.

9 Sprinkle 1-2 teaspoons of the remaining sugar over each ramekin so that it thinly covers the surface. Place under the hot grill to caramelise the sugar and leave to set.

COFFEE MOUSSE

Prep and cook time: 40 min plus 4 hours chilling
Serves 4

150g milk chocolate, at least 30% cocoa solids

2 leaves gelatine

4 tbsp instant coffee powder

300 ml whipping cream

2 fresh eggs

1½ tbsp coffee liqueur

Pinch of salt

2½ tbsp sugar

Whipped cream, to serve

Cocoa powder, to decorate

1 Break up the chocolate and melt in a bowl standing over a pan of simmering water. Soak the gelatine in cold water. Mix the coffee powder with 100 ml of the cream.

2 Separate 1 egg and beat the egg yolk and the whole egg with the coffee cream in a bowl standing over a pan of simmering water, until thick and creamy. Squeeze out the gelatine and stir into the mixture until dissolved. Remove the bowl from the heat and add the chocolate and coffee liqueur. Stir until cold.

3 Whisk the egg white with a pinch of salt until stiff, trickling in the sugar at the same time. Whisk the remaining cream until stiff and fold both into the coffee mixture.

4 Divide the mousse between 4 dishes and chill in the refrigerator for at least 4 hours.

5 To serve, add a topping of whipped cream and dust with cocoa powder to decorate.

TIRAMISÙ

Prep and cook time: 30 min plus 6 hours chilling time
Serves 4

5 fresh egg yolks

50g icing sugar

500g mascarpone

3 tbsp almond liqueur

500 ml strong espresso

16 sponge fingers

Cocoa powder, for dusting

Icing sugar, for dusting

1 Beat the egg yolks and icing sugar until foaming, then stir in the mascarpone and the liqueur.

2 Pour the espresso into a flat dish. Quickly dip half of the sponge fingers in the espresso and lay them on the base of a rectangular serving dish.

3 Spread the sponge fingers with half of the egg and marscapone cream mixture and dust with cocoa. Repeat the process with the remaining sponge fingers and mascarpone cream. Dust with cocoa and icing sugar and chill for a few hours or overnight before serving.

SEASONAL BAKING

APPLE NUT CAKE

Prep and cook time: 1 hour 20 min

150g soft butter

150g sugar

1 tsp vanilla extract

4 eggs

250g plain flour

1 tsp baking powder

Pinch of salt

750g apples

100g cold butter

3 tbsp sugar

80g chopped pecans

8–10 pecan halves

Icing sugar, for dusting

1 Preheat the oven to 180°C / 350°F / Gas Mark 4. Grease a 26-cm spring-release cake tin.

2 Put the butter, sugar and vanilla extract in a large bowl and beat together until light and fluffy. Beat in the eggs. Sift in the flour, baking powder and salt and stir into the mixture.

3 Peel, quarter and core the apples. Coarsely grate 1 apple and stir into the batter. Halve the remaining apple quarters lengthways. Turn the batter into the prepared cake tin.

4 Arrange the apples on top of the batter, pressing in lightly, dot with butter and scatter the chopped pecans around the edge. Sprinkle with the sugar and arrange the pecan halves in the middle of the cake.

5 Bake in the oven for about 50 minutes. Leave to cool in the cake tin before serving, dusted with icing sugar.

APPLE CRUMBLE CAKE

Prep and cook time: 1 hour 40 min

125g butter, plus extra for greasing

125g sugar

3 eggs

1 tsp vanilla essence

125g quark or low-fat cream cheese

3 tbsp cornflour

1½ tsp baking powder

200g plain flour

600g apples, peeled, cored and chopped

For the crumble:

75g butter

75g plain flour

75g ground almonds

2 tbsp sugar

1 tsp cinnamon

1 Preheat the oven to 180°C / 350°F / Gas Mark 4. Butter a 26-cm spring-release cake tin.

2 Beat the butter and sugar together until light and fluffy. Beat in the eggs, one at a time, and then add the vanilla essence and the cheese and mix well together. Sift in the cornflour, baking powder and flour and stir into the mixture.

3 Fold the chopped apples into the batter. Turn the batter into the prepared cake pan.

4 To make the crumble, melt the butter. Mix the flour, ground almonds, sugar and cinnamon together and add the melted butter. Mix to a crumbly mixture and scatter on top of the cake.

5 Bake in the oven for 40–50 minutes, until golden brown. Leave to cool in the tin before serving.

APPLE SCONES

Prep and cook time: 30 min   Makes 8

225g plain flour

2 tsp baking powder

1 tsp bicarbonate of soda

Pinch of salt

3 tbsp caster sugar

50g butter

1 apple, peeled, cored and finely chopped

1 egg

75 ml milk, plus extra to glaze

1 Preheat the oven to 230°C /450°F / Gas Mark 8. Place an ungreased baking sheet in the oven to heat.

2 Sift the flour, baking powder, bicarbonate of soda, salt and 2 tbsp of the sugar into a large bowl.

3 Cut the butter into cubes, add to the flour mixture and rub in with your fingertips until the mixture forms crumbs.

4 Add the apple to the dry ingredients and stir to coat the pieces in the flour mixture.

5 Put the egg and milk in a jug and mix together with a fork. Gradually pour into the flour mixture and bring everything together with your hands to make a soft, manageable dough.

6 Roll out the dough on a lightly floured surface to a thickness of about 2cm. Using a 5-cm plain cutter, stamp out 8 rounds.

7 Use a palette knife to lift the scones on to the preheated baking sheet. Brush with milk and sprinkle with the remaining sugar.

8 Bake in the oven for 8–10 minutes until well risen, firm and pale golden. Leave to cool on a wire rack.

An apple a day keeps the doctor away

APPLE CAKES

Prep and cook time: 25 min Makes 12

2 eggs

110g caster sugar

110g self-raising flour

110g butter, melted

1 apple, peeled and diced

Icing sugar to decorate

1   Heat the oven to 180°C / 350°F / Gas Mark 4. Grease a 12-hole cake or bun tin.

2   Whisk the eggs and sugar together in a bowl until light and fluffy.

3   Gently fold in the flour and butter, followed by the apple.

4   Divide the mixture between the holes of the bun tin and bake for 8–10 minutes, until golden brown and a skewer inserted into one of the cakes comes out clean. Leave in the tins for 10 minutes, and then place on a wire rack to cool.

5   Sift a little icing sugar over the tops just before serving.

Marvellous Muffins

RASPBERRY AND COCONUT MUFFINS

Prep and cook time: 35 min   Makes 12

225g plain flour

1 tbsp baking powder

110g sugar

2 eggs

120g butter, melted

175 ml milk

175g sweetened shredded coconut

110g fresh raspberries

Icing sugar for dusting

1   Heat the oven to 180°C / 350°F / Gas Mark 4. Grease a 12-hole muffin tin.

2   Sift the flour and baking powder into a mixing bowl and stir in the sugar.

3   Mix together the eggs, butter and milk until combined. Stir into the dry ingredients until only just mixed and still slightly lumpy.

4   Gently stir in the coconut and raspberries. Spoon the mixture into the muffin tin, filling each hole three-quarters full.

5   Bake for 20–25 minutes until golden and risen.

6   Leave in to stand for 3 minutes, and then place on a wire rack to cool.

7   Sift icing sugar over the muffins just before serving.

BLACKBERRY AND RASPBERRY MUFFINS

Prep and cook time: 35 min   Makes 12

175g plain flour

2 tsp baking powder

110g sugar

110g butter, melted

1 egg

120 ml milk

110g blackberries

110g raspberries

For the topping:

50g finely chopped almonds

50g sugar

3 tbsp flour

45g butter, melted

1   Heat the oven to 180°C / 350°F / Gas Mark 4. Grease a 12-cup muffin tin.

2   Sift the flour and baking powder into a mixing bowl and stir in the sugar.

3   Beat the melted butter with the egg and milk and gradually stir into the dry ingredients until just mixed but still slightly lumpy.

4   Gently stir in the blackberries and raspberries.

5   Spoon the mixture into the muffin cups, filling almost to the top.

6   For the topping, mix all the ingredients together and spoon a little over the top of each muffin.

7   Bake for about 25 minutes until risen and firm.

8   Leave to stand for 5 minutes, then place on a wire rack to cool.

CHERRY CRUMBLE MUFFINS

Prep and cook time: 45 min   Makes 12

90g butter

350g plain flour

4 tsp baking powder

200g caster sugar

Finely grated zest 1 lemon

150g pitted sweet fresh or frozen cherries

2 eggs

250 ml milk

175g cream cheese

25g ground almonds

1   Preheat the oven to 200°C / 400°F / Gas Mark 6. Line a 12- hole muffin tin with paper muffin cases.

2   Melt 75g the butter. Sift the flour and baking powder into a large bowl. Add a heaped 125g of sugar, the lemon zest and the cherries. Stir together to coat the cherries in the flour.

3   Put the eggs and melted butter in a jug and mix together with a fork.

4   Add the liquid ingredients to the flour mixture and stir together until just combined.

5   Melt the remaining butter and set aside.

6   Put the cream cheese in a bowl and mix in 2 tbsp of sugar.

7   Divide half the muffin mixture equally between the muffin cases. Spoon a dollop of cream cheese into each one. Top with the remaining muffin mixture.

8   Add the remaining sugar and the ground almonds to the remaining melted butter and mix together. Sprinkle the crumble mixture over the top of each muffin.

9   Bake in the oven for 15 minutes until the muffins are well risen and firm. Leave to cool on a wire rack.

PLUM AND ALMOND MUFFINS

Prep and cook time: 35 min   Makes 12

175g caster sugar

150 ml light oil

1 egg

100 ml milk

1 tsp almond extract

200g plain flour

1 tbsp baking powder

75g ground almonds

200g plums, quartered and stoned

1   Preheat the oven to 190°C / 375°F / Gas Mark 5. Line a 12-hole muffin tin with paper muffin cases or generously grease the cups.

2   Put the sugar, oil, egg, milk and almond extract in a jug and mix together with a fork.

3   Sift the flour and baking powder into a large bowl. Add the ground almonds and mix together.

4   Add the plums to the flour mixture and toss together to coat the plums in the flour.

5   Add the liquid ingredients to the flour mixture and stir together until just combined.

6   Spoon the mixture evenly between the muffin cases or prepared cups.

7   Bake in the oven for 15–20 minutes until the muffins are pale golden brown, risen and firm. Leave to cool on a wire rack.

Sugar and spice and all things nice

APPLE AND CINNAMON MUFFINS

Prep and cook time: 40 min Makes 8

125g butter, softened

125g caster sugar

2 large eggs

125g plain flour

1 tsp baking powder

½ tsp bicarbonate of soda

1 tsp cinnamon

100g apple sauce

1 tsp cinnamon

For the icing:

200g icing sugar

About 5 tbsp milk

1 tsp vanilla extract

½ tsp cinnamon

1 apple

2 tbsp lemon juice

1 Preheat the oven to 180°C / 350°F/ Gas Mark 4. Line an 8-hole muffin tin with paper cases.

2 Put the butter and sugar in a large bowl and, using a hand-held electric whisk, beat together until light and fluffy.

3 Add the eggs to the mixture, one at a time, beating thoroughly after each addition.

4 Sift in the flour, baking powder, bicarbonate of soda and cinnamon. Add the apple sauce and stir everything together until combined.

5 Divide the mixture equally between the muffin cases.

6 Bake in the oven for 25 minutes until firm or a cocktail stick inserted into the centre comes out clean. Leave to cool on a wire rack.

7 To make the topping, sift the icing sugar into a large bowl. Add the milk and vanilla and mix until smooth. If the icing is too stiff, add a little extra milk. Spoon the icing on top of the muffins, allowing it to drizzle down the sides.

8 Core, quarter and slice the apple. Toss the slices in the lemon juice. Sprinkle the cinnamon over the muffins and top with the apple pieces.

GINGERBREAD MUFFINS

Prep and cook time: 40 min Makes 12

115g butter

250g plain flour

225g caster sugar

2 tsp baking powder

2 tsp ground ginger

½ tsp ground cinnamon

2 eggs

3 tbsp honey

3 tbsp ginger syrup and 2 tbsp chopped preserved ginger

175 ml hot water

Icing sugar, to decorate

1 Preheat the oven to 180°C / 350°F/ Gas Mark 4. Grease a 12-hole muffin tin.

2 Melt the butter. Sift the flour, sugar, baking powder, ginger and cinnamon into a large bowl.

3 Beat together the eggs, honey, ginger syrup and butter until smooth. Stir into the dry ingredients.

4 Add the water and chopped ginger and stir well until combined. Spoon the mixture equally into the muffin cups.

5 Bake in the oven for 20–25 minutes until golden brown and a skewer inserted into the centre comes out clean. Leave in the tin for 10 minutes and then transfer to a wire rack and leave to cool.

6 Sift a little icing sugar over the muffins to decorate just before serving.

GINGERBREAD BUNDT CAKE

Prep and cook time: 1 hour 30 min plus 2 hours chilling time

250g soft butter

250g sugar

5 eggs

500g plain flour

½ tsp salt

3 tsp baking powder

2 tsp gingerbread, apple pie or mixed spice

3 tbsp cocoa powder

250 ml milk

For the icing:

2 tbsp cream cheese

5 tbsp whipping cream

5 tbsp icing sugar

1 Preheat the oven to 170°C / 325°F / Gas Mark 3. Grease a bundt cake mould.

2 Put the butter and sugar in a large bowl and beat together until light and fluffy. Add the eggs and beat until pale and creamy. Sift in the flour, salt, baking powder, spice and cocoa powder and stir into the mixture. Gradually stir in enough milk to produce a soft batter. Turn the batter into the prepared cake mould.

3 Bake in the oven for about 1 hour, until a wooden cocktail stick inserted into the middle comes out clean. Cover with foil if it browns too quickly. Turn out on to a wire rack and leave to cool.

4 To make the icing, put the cream cheese and cream in a large bowl and mix together. Add the icing sugar and mix well. Drizzle the frosting over the cold cake and chill for 1–2 hours before serving.

SPICED RAISIN CAKE

Prep and cook time: 1 hour 25 min

150g butter, plus extra for greasing

2 tbsp cocoa powder, plus extra for dusting

100g sugar

8 eggs, separated

250g plain flour

200g raisins

1 tbsp cinnamon

Large pinch ground cloves

150 ml whipping cream

1 tsp vanilla essence

Cinnamon, for spinkling

1 Preheat the oven to 180°C / 350°F/ Gas Mark 4. Butter a 30 x 11.5cm loaf tin and dust with cocoa powder.

2 Melt the butter and leave to cool slightly. Add the sugar to the egg yolks and beat together until foamy. Stir in the butter, then one after the other stir the flour, cocoa powder, raisins, cinnamon and cloves into the mixture.

3 Whisk the egg whites until stiff and carefully fold into the batter. Turn the batter into the prepared loaf tin and smooth the top.

4 Bake in the oven for about 1 hour. Leave to cool slightly in the tin, and then remove from the tin and leave to cool completely.

5 To serve, whisk the cream with vanilla essence until stiff. Spread on top of the cake and sprinkle with cinnamon.

PUMPKIN AND WALNUT LOAF

Prep and cook time: 1 hour 15 min

300g pumpkin, peeled, deseeded and grated

1 banana, mashed

375g plain flour

¼ tsp salt

2 tsp baking powder

½ tsp bicarbonate of soda

2 tsp cinnamon

175g butter

125g light soft brown sugar

150g runny honey

1 egg

100g chopped walnuts

1 Preheat the oven to 180°C / 350°F/ Gas Mark 4. Grease and line a 900g loaf tin with greaseproof paper.

2 Loosely combine the pumpkin and banana with a fork and set aside.

3 Sift the flour, salt, baking powder, bicarbonate of soda and cinnamon into a small bowl and set aside.

4 In a large bowl cream the butter and sugar until smooth. Add the honey and egg, mixing until the mixture becomes loose. Add the pumpkin/ banana mixture.

5 Stir in the flour mixture in 3 parts, adding the walnuts just as the flour is combined. Do not over mix. Turn the mixture into the prepared loaf tin.

5 Bake the loaf in the oven for 45–50 minutes until risen and firm to the touch. Insert a cocktail stick into the centre of the loaf and if it comes out clean the loaf is cooked. Cool in the pan for 5 minutes, then turn out and leave to cool on a wire rack.

CRANBERRY BREAD

Prep and cook time: 1 hour 20 min

Flour for dusting the tin

45g butter

100g buckwheat flour

100g wholemeal flour

75g ground almonds

1 tsp baking powder

100g caster sugar

50g soft brown sugar

125g fresh or dried cranberries

2 large eggs

125 ml orange juice

4 tbsp natural yoghurt

1 tsp grated orange zest

1 Preheat the oven to 180°C / 350°F/ Gas Mark 4. Grease and flour a 900g loaf tin.

2 Melt the butter and set aside. Put the buckwheat and wholemeal flour into a large bowl. Add the ground almonds and baking powder.

3 Add the caster sugar, brown sugar and cranberries to the flour mixture and stir together.

4 Break the eggs into a jug and beat with a fork until frothy. Gradually stir in the orange juice, yoghurt, orange zest and melted butter.

5 Pour the liquid ingredients into the flour mixture and stir to combine.

6 Pour the batter into the prepared loaf tin.

7 Bake in the oven for 1 hour until firm to the touch, or a cocktail stick inserted into the centre comes out clean. Leave to cool on a wire rack and serve sliced.

MINI CHOCOLATE MUFFINS

Prep and cook time: 30 mins Makes 24 mini muffins

100g grated plain chocolate (60% cocoa solids)

100g butter

75g sugar

1 tsp vanilla extract

1 pinch salt

1 egg

200g plain flour

1 tsp baking powder

½ tsp bicarbonate of (baking) soda

1 tbsp cocoa powder

100 ml milk

50g chopped peanuts

1   Heat the oven to 180°C /350°F/ Gas Mark 4. Line a 24-hole mini muffin tin with paper baking cases.

2   Beat together the chocolate and butter in a mixing bowl until soft and creamy.

3   Gradually beat in the sugar, vanilla and salt until smooth.

4   Beat in the egg until incorporated. Gradually sift in the flour, baking powder, bicarbonate of soda and cocoa and fold in gently, alternating with the milk, until well blended. Fold in the peanuts.

5   Spoon into the paper cases and bake for 15–20 minutes, until springy to the touch. Cool in the tins for 10 minutes, then place on a wire rack to cool completely.

ALMOND BROWNIES

Prep and cook time: 1 hr

Oil, for greasing the baking tin

100g plain chocolate (50% cocoa solids)

125g soft butter

150g brown sugar

2 eggs

100g plain flour

½ tsp baking powder

Salt

1 tsp vanilla essence

150g flaked almonds

Icing sugar, for dusting

1   Preheat the oven to to 200°C / 400°F / Gas Mark 6. Grease a baking tin.

2   Roughly chop the chocolate and melt over a bowl of simmering water, then set aside.

3   Put the butter and brown sugar into a bowl and cream with an electric mixer until light and fluffy. Beat in the eggs and stir in the melted chocolate.

4   Mix the flour with the baking powder, a pinch of salt and the vanilla essence. Stir the almonds into the brownie batter with the flour.

5   Turn the batter into the pan and bake for 30–40 minutes, or until a wooden cocktail stick inserted into the middle comes out clean. Turn out onto a rack and let cool completely. Dust with icing sugar and cut into pieces to serve.

CHOCOLATE AND BANANA MUFFINS

Prep and cook time: 45 min   Makes 6

120g butter, melted, plus extra to grease the tin

120g self-raising flour

120g sugar

1 tsp bicarbonate of soda

Pinch of salt

½ tsp ground cinnamon

100g plain chocolate (70% cocoa solids), chopped

1 egg, beaten

1 tsp vanilla essence

2 very ripe bananas

For the topping:

6 banana slices

Melted butter

1   Heat the oven to 180°C / 350°F/ Gas Mark 4. Grease a 6-hole muffin tin.

2   Sift the flour, sugar, bicarbonate of soda, salt and cinnamon into a mixing bowl. Stir in the chopped chocolate.

3   Make a well in the centre and add the beaten egg, warm butter and vanilla essence.

4   Mash the bananas well and stir into the mixture until just combined, but still slightly lumpy.

5   Spoon the mixture into the holes of the muffin tin and top each with a slice of banana. Brush the banana slices with a little melted butter.

6   Bake for 25–30 minutes until firm and risen. Leave in the tin for 5 minutes, then place on a wire rack to cool.

CELEBRATE

MULLED WINE

Prep and cook time: 20 min   Serves 12

2 unwaxed oranges

Peel from 1 lemon

150g caster sugar

Pinch dried ginger

Pinch of freshly grated
nutmeg

1 cinnamon stick

5 cardamom pods (optional)

2 bottles of fruity red wine

Dried cloves

1   Juice one of the oranges and add the juice to a large saucepan
with the lemon peel, sugar and spices. Add enough wine to cover the
sugar and heat gently, stirring regularly, until the sugar dissolves.

2   Bring the mixture to the boil and cook for about 5 minutes, until it
has reduced to a thick syrup.

3   Meanwhile, stud the second orange with vertical lines of cloves at
regular intervals. Cut into segments.

4   Turn down the heat down and add the remainder of the wine to
the syrup in the saucepan. Add the orange segments. Gently heat the
mixture through – do not allow it to boil.

5   Serve warm with the orange segments as a garnish.

WARM APPLE PUNCH

Prep and cook time: 30 min Serves 6

1.5 litres apple juice

3 cinnamon stick

10 juniper berries

Zest and juice of 3 oranges
cinnamon sticks, to garnish

Red apple peel, to garnish

1   Put the apple juice, cinnamon stick and
juniper berries into a large saucepan.

2   Add the orange juice and zest to the
saucepan; bring to a boil, reduce the heat and
simmer for 20 minutes to infuse the spices.

3   Strain the punch and ladle into heatproof
glasses. Garnish each with a cinnamon stick
and a swirl of apple peel.

KIR ROYALE

Prep time: 5 min Serves 6

Bottle Champagne or Cava, chilled

Splash crème de cassis per glass

1   Pour chilled champagne into six champagne flutes to nearly
fill, leaving a little space below the rim.

2   Add a splash of the crème de cassis to taste and serve
immediately.

CHILLI MANGO COCKTAIL

Prep time: 15 min   Serves 6

3 red chillies, sliced and deseeded

90 ml lime juice

180 ml agave syrup

300 ml elderflower cordial (made up from 90–130 ml of undiluted cordial plus cold water)

1.35 litres mango juice

8 handfuls ice cubes

180 ml grenadine

Red chillies and sticks of fresh mango to garnish

1   Put all the chilli slices into a cocktail shaker and mash with a long spoon.

2   Add the lime juice, agave syrup, 100 ml of the elderflower cordial, 450 ml of the mango juice and 2 handfuls of the ice.

3   Shake the cocktail shaker well and strain the juice into a jug. Add the remaining elderflower cordial and mango juice and stir well.

4   Put about 4 tablespoons grenadine and a handful of ice into each of six tall glasses. Top each glass up with the cocktail mixture.

5   Garnish each glass with a chilli and a stick of mango.

ICED FRUIT COCKTAIL

Prep time: 15 min   Serves 6

600g mixed fruit (try grapefruit, apple, black grapes) cut into bite-size pieces

750 ml apple juice

90 ml lime juice

18 ice cubes

About 600 ml well-chilled sparkling mineral water

1   Thread the prepared fruit onto six long, round-ended wooden skewers.

2   Pour the apple juice and lime juice into a blender. Add the ice cubes and pulse briefly.

3   Divide the juice mixture between six tall glasses and add a fruit skewer to each. Top up each glass with mineral water.

> Add some sparkle to any occasion with delicious alcohol-free cocktails

LIME MARGARITAS

Prep time: 15 min   Serves 6

6 large limes

About 6 tsp sea salt

150 ml pressed apple juice

450 ml white grape juice

Crushed ice, as needed

1   Finely grate the zest from the limes; reserve half for garnish and put the rest into a blender.

2   Juice the limes. Pour about 3 tablespoons of the lime juice into a saucer and the sea salt into another.

3   Dip the rim of an upturned margarita glass into the lime juice, then into the salt. Repeat with the other five glasses.

4   Put the remaining lime juice into the blender with the apple juice, grape juice and ice. Blend until slushy.

5   Divide the mixture between the salt-rimmed glasses and sprinkle with reserved lime zest. Serve immediately.

LEMON GRASS LEMONADE

Prep time: 15 min plus 8 hrs chill time   Serves 6

3 stems lemon grass

Zest and juice of 6 large lemons

150g caster sugar

1.75 litres boiling water

Ice cubes

Lemon grass stems and mint sprigs to garnish

1   Trim off the base and top of the three lemon grass stems and finely slice. Put the sliced lemon grass into a large heatproof jug and add the lemon juice, zest and sugar.

2   Pour the boiling water into the jug. Cover and leave to steep overnight.

3   Stir and taste for sweetness, adding more sugar if needed. Strain the lemonade into six glasses.

4   Top up each glass with ice cubes and garnish with a lemon grass stem and a sprig of mint.

SMOKED MACKEREL AND HORSERADISH PÂTÉ

Prep and cook time: 10 min plus 2 hours to chill

450g smoked mackerel

225g crème fraîche

2 tbsp ready-made creamed horseradish

Pepper

1 In a food processor, blend the mackerel, crème fraîche and creamed horseradish to a smooth consistency. Season with pepper, spoon into four small dishes and chill for at least 2 hours.

Delicious dips are easy to whip up – team with sliced raw vegetables, strips of pitta bread or tortilla for instant party style

CREAMY RED PEPPER DIP

Prep and cook time: 30 min

3 red peppers

1 red chilli pepper, deseeded and chopped

1 clove garlic, peeled and roughly chopped

250g full fat cream cheese

2 tbsp mayonnaise

2 tbsp olive oil

¼ tsp paprika, to garnish

Rosemary leaves, to garnish

Red chilli pepper, to garnish

1 Place the peppers under a hot grill and cook until the skins start to blacken and blister, turning from time to time. Let cool.

2 Carefully remove the blackened skins and scrape out the seeds.

3 Put the peppers and all the other ingredients into a food processor and blend until smooth; add a little water if the mix is too stiff.

4 Season with salt and pepper and garnish with a few slices of chilli pepper, rosemary leaves and a pinch of paprika.

BEET HUMMUS

Prep and cook time: 1 hour 30 min plus 12 hrs soaking time

300g chickpeas

1 medium beetroot, peeled and cut into 2cm cubes

150g tahini (sesame paste)

Juice of 1 lemon

2 tbsp olive oil

3 cloves garlic

1 pinch cumin

Salt, to taste

1   Soak the chickpeas in water overnight.

2   Drain and place the chickpeas in a saucepan; add enough water to cover by 5cm. Bring to a boil, reduce the heat and simmer until the chickpeas are barely tender, about 40 minutes. Add the cubed beetroot and continue cooking until tender. Drain and rinse in a colander under cold running water.

3   Purée the chickpeas and beetroot, tahini, lemon juice, oil, garlic and cumin in a food processor or blender; season with salt. Transfer to a serving bowl, cover and chill for about 30 minutes.

For a quicker version, drain a 400g tin of chickpeas and mix with a chopped precooked beetroot; skip steps 1 and 2.

BABA GHANOUSH

Prep and cook time: 45 min

1 kg aubergine

1 small onion, coarsely chopped

2 tsp chopped fresh parsley

3–4 cloves garlic, chopped

About 120 ml olive oil

Salt and pepper, to taste

3–6 tbsp lemon juice

1   Preheat the grill (or preheat the oven to 200°C / 400°F /Gas Mark 6). Pierce the aubergines in several places with a fork. Grill or bake until the skin blisters and wrinkles and the flesh is soft. Leave to cool, then halve lengthwise and scrape out the flesh, discarding the skin.

2   Roughly chop the aubergine flesh and purée in a blender or food processor with the onion, parsley and garlic. Stir in enough olive oil to produce a creamy paste. Season with salt and pepper and add lemon juice to taste. Spoon into a bowl, cover and chill.

FRIED CHORIZO WITH TOMATO AND ONION SAUCE

Prep and cook time: 20 min

6 large tomatoes

125 ml olive oil

250g cooking chorizo, sliced

1 large onion, chopped

1 garlic clove

2 stalks thyme

Salt and freshly ground pepper

1   Bring a pan of salted water to a boil and drop in the tomatoes for 30 seconds. Remove from the water, peel and slice. Set aside.

2   Heat 4 tablespoons of the oil in a wide pan and fry the chorizo slices for about 5 minutes, turning once. Set aside.

3   Heat the remaining oil in the pan and gently cook the onion until soft. Add the garlic, cook for 2 minutes then add the tomatoes.

4   Cover the pan and simmer for 8 minutes, adding a little water if necessary.

5   Add the chorizo and the thyme sprigs and cook for a further 3 minutes. Season with salt and pepper and serve.

CHICKEN WITH RED PEPPER SAUCE

Prep and cook time: 45 min   Makes 10 pieces

125 ml oil

Juice of 2 limes

2 tbsp honey

1 red chilli, seeds removed and chopped

2 chicken breasts, skinned

2 orange peppers

1 garlic clove

Salt and freshly ground pepper

Lime zest, to garnish

1   Whisk together 6 tablespoons of the oil with the lime juice, honey and chopped chilli to make a marinade.

2   Cut the chicken into bite-size pieces, mix with the marinade and set aside.

3   Brush the peppers with a little oil and place under a hot grill until the skins are charred all over, turning frequently. Put in a bowl, cover with cling film and set aside.

4   Heat 2 tablespoons of oil in a pan and gently fry the garlic for 2 minutes.

5   Remove and discard the pepper skins and seeds. Place the peppers in a food processor with the garlic and blend well. Season with salt and pepper and set aside.

6   Remove the chicken from the marinade. Heat the remaining oil in a frying pan and fry the chicken pieces for about 6 minutes or until browned on all sides and cooked through.

7   Mix the peppers and garlic with the reserved marinade, briskly bring to a boil in the frying pan then turn down the heat. Drizzle over the chicken pieces. Scatter with lime zest and serve immediately.

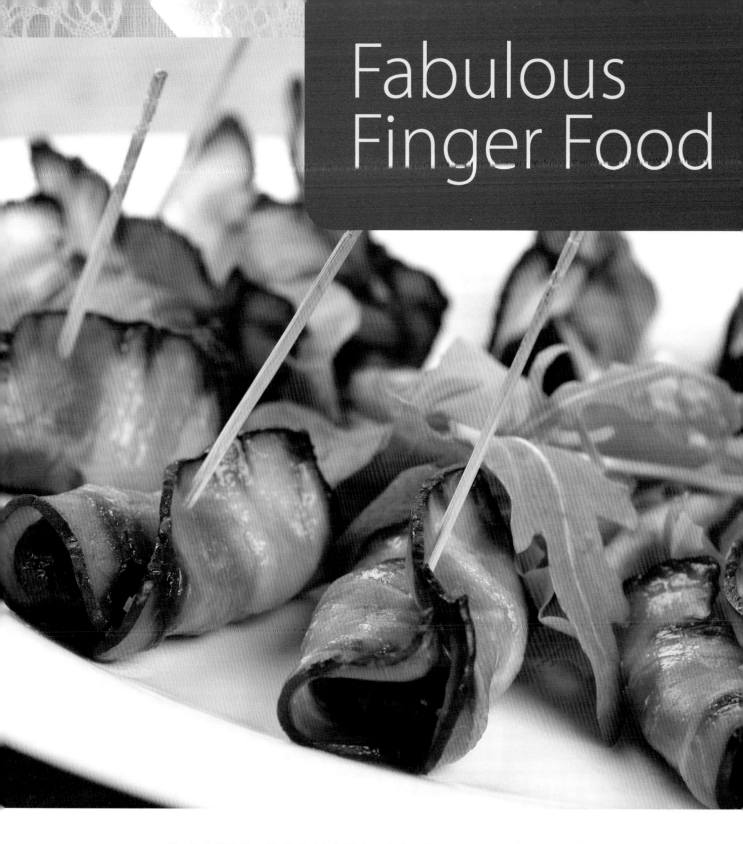

BAKED PRUNES AND ALMONDS WRAPPED IN BACON

Prep and cook time: 25 min   Makes 24

24 whole almonds, skinned

24 prunes, pitted

12 slices bacon, halved

2 tbsp oil

1   Heat the oven to 200°C / 400°F / Gas Mark 6.

2   Place an almond in the cavity of each prune, wrap in a piece of bacon and secure with a wooden cocktail stick.

3   Place the wrapped prunes on a baking tray, drizzle with the oil and bake for 10–15 minutes.

TOMATO AND BREAD SKEWERS ON PARMA HAM

Prep and cook time: 15 min   Makes 8

3–4 thick slices white bread, cut into 3-cm cubes

2 cloves garlic

50 ml olive oil

16 cherry tomatoes

2 sprigs thyme, leaves

6–8 small gherkins

8 slices Parma ham

2 tbsp extra virgin olive oil

1 tbsp lemon juice

Salt and coarsely milled pepper

1 Purée the garlic finely with the oil and briefly toss the bread cubes in the flavoured oil. Preheat the grill.

2 Thread the tomatoes on wooden skewers with the bread, alternating tomatoes with bread. Sprinkle with thyme.

3 Cook on all sides under a hot grill for about 5 minutes.

4 Drain the gherkins, slice lengthways and put on a plate with the Parma ham. Mix the oil with the lemon juice and sprinkle over the gherkins and ham. Arrange the skewers on top and season lightly with pepper and salt. Serve at once.

SHRIMP AND TOMATO KEBABS WITH THAI SAUCE

Prep and cook time: 20 min plus 30 min to marinate   Makes 24

6 tbsp soy sauce

2 tbsp fish sauce

3 tbsp sesame oil

Juice of 2 limes

2 tbsp honey

2 red chillies, seeds removed and finely chopped

2 garlic cloves, finely chopped

2 spring onions, finely chopped

675g large prawns, tails and black veins removed

450g cherry tomatoes, halved

Lime wedges, to garnish

1   Mix the soy sauce, fish sauce, 2 tbsp of the sesame oil, the lime juice and honey in a large bowl.

2   Add the chopped chillies, garlic and spring onions and mix in the prawns. Set aside to marinate for 30 minutes, turning from time to time.

3   Heat the grill to a medium setting.

4   Remove the prawns from the marinade, brush the tomato halves with the remaining oil and thread onto wooden skewers alternating with the prawns.

5   Heat the marinade in a small pan until reduced and slightly sticky. Set aside.

6   Cook the kebabs under the grill, turning frequently, for about 6 minutes or until the prawns are cooked through.

7   Serve the kebabs with the warm marinade drizzled over and lime wedges to garnish.

APPLE AND CELERIAC SALAD

Prep and cook time: 20 min

400–500g celeriac	300g low-fat yogurt
3–4 apples	Salt and pepper
3 tbsp lemon juice	1 pinch sugar
2 sprigs parsley	

1 Peel the celeriac and cut into slices. Cook in boiling, salted water for about 3 minutes. Drain, place immediately into cold water, then drain again.

2 Peel and quarter the apples and remove the core. Cut into thin slices. Drizzle lemon juice over the apples. Cut the slices of celeriac into thin sticks and mix with the apples.

3 Chop the parsley into thin strips.

4 Season the yoghurt with salt, pepper, and a pinch of sugar, then add to the apple and celeriac and stir well. Season to taste and sprinkle the parsley over the top.

BEAN SALAD WITH ONIONS AND TOMATOES

Prep and cook time: 20 min

6 tbsp olive oil	500g cherry tomatoes, halved
100 ml vegetable stock	150g canned small white beans (eg haricot), rinsed and drained
4 tbsp white wine vinegar	2 red onions, thinly sliced
½ tsp dry mustard	Fresh parsley leaves, for garnish
Salt and freshly ground pepper	

1 In a medium bowl, whisk the oil, stock, vinegar and mustard to make a vinaigrette; season with salt and pepper.

2 Add the tomatoes, beans and onions and toss to coat. Let stand 20 minutes to marinate.

3 Sprinkle a few parsley leaves over the salad before serving.

CLASSIC POTATO SALAD

Prep and cook time: 50 min

800g boiling potatoes

4 tbsp sour cream

2 tbsp mayonnaise

4–5 tbsp vegetable stock

White wine vinegar, to taste

2 spring onions, finely chopped

Salt, to taste

1 red onion, sliced

1 handful fresh herbs, e. g. parsley or cress

2 tbsp capers

1 Place the potatoes in a steamer basket; set in a saucepan over 3cm of boiling water. Cover and steam until tender, about 25 minutes. Drain and return to the hot pan to dry briefly, then peel and slice. Allow the potatoes to cool for a few minutes.

2 Mix the sour cream, mayonnaise, stock and vinegar in a large bowl; add the spring onions and season to taste with salt. Add the potatoes and onion and toss gently to coat. Scatter the herbs and capers over the salad and serve.

WARM POTATO SALAD

Prep and cook time: 50 min

400g cherry tomatoes

salt and black pepper

1 tsp sugar

6 tbsp olive oil

1–2 tbsp balsamic vinegar

2 red onions, sliced

900g unpeeled potatoes, thickly sliced

50 g sun-dried tomatoes in oil, drained and thinly sliced

1 tbsp olive oil

1 tbsp chopped flat-leaf parsley

1 Heat the oven to 180°C / 350°F / Gas Mark 4. Line a baking tray with non-stick baking paper.

2 Arrange the cherry tomatoes in a single layer on the baking tray. Sprinkle lightly with salt and the sugar, then drizzle 2 tablespoons oil and the balsamic vinegar over the top. Cook for about 20 minutes until tender.

3 Heat the remaining oil in a frying pan and cook the onions over a medium heat for 5–8 minutes, until lightly caramelised.

4 Bring a pan of salted water to a boil and cook the potatoes for about 10 minutes, until just cooked through. Drain well.

5 Toss all the vegetables together and season to taste with salt and freshly ground black pepper. Place in a warmed serving dish. Drizzle with the oil and sprinkle with the parsley.

HONEY AND MUSTARD CHICKEN WINGS WITH SESAME SEEDS

**Prep and cook time: 30 min plus 1 hour marinating time
Makes 12**

3 tbsp olive oil

4 tbsp honey

2 tbsp Dijon mustard

Juice of 1 lemon

Salt and freshly ground pepper

12 chicken wings

4 tbsp sesame seeds

1   Whisk together the oil, honey, mustard and lemon juice to make a marinade. Season with salt and pepper.

2   Put the chicken wings into a large bowl, pour over the marinade and mix well. Set aside for at least 1 hour, turning from time to time.

3   Heat the oven to 200°C / 400°F / Gas Mark 6.

4   Toast the sesame seeds in a dry frying pan until lightly browned. Set aside.

5   Remove the chicken wings from the marinade and put onto a baking tray. Roast in the oven for 15–20 minutes, turning once, until cooked through and browned all over.

6   Sprinkle the chicken wings with the toasted sesame seeds and serve warm or cold.

POTATO TORTILLA

Prep and cook time: 50 min

4 medium waxy potatoes, peeled

6 eggs

1 tbsp thyme, finely chopped

2 tbsp parsley, finely chopped

Salt and freshly ground pepper

4 tbsp olive oil

1   Boil the potatoes in a large pan of salted water until just tender. Let cool a little, cut in half lengthways and slice.

2   Beat the eggs in a large bowl, add the herbs, season with salt and pepper and add the sliced potatoes.

3   Heat 2 tablespoons of oil over a medium flame in a 20-cm frying pan and pour in half the egg/potato mixture.

4   Allow to cook for about 3 minutes then place a large plate over the pan, carefully invert and slide the tortilla, uncooked side down, back into the frying pan.

5   Continue cooking for 2 more minutes or until the mixture is set, then remove the tortilla from the pan.

6   Repeat with the remaining oil and egg/potato mixture. Slice the tortillas and serve warm or cold.

POTATOES BAKED IN SALT WITH SOUR CREAM AND 'CAVIAR'

Prep and cook time: 1 hour

12 small new potatoes

2 tbsp olive oil

250g rock salt

250 ml sour cream

125g salmon caviar or lump fish roe

Zest of two lemons

Dill sprigs, to garnish

1 Heat the oven to 180°C / 350°F / Gas Mark 4.

2 Wash the potatoes thoroughly and rub with the oil.

3 Scatter some of the rock salt onto a baking tray and place the potatoes on top. Bake in the oven for 45 minutes or until the potatoes are tender.

4 Scatter some of the salt onto a serving dish. Slice open the potatoes, place onto the serving dish and spoon a little soured cream into each one.

5 Top the potatoes with the fish roe, drizzle over any remaining cream, scatter over the lemon zest and garnish with dill sprigs.

MINI QUICHES WITH MUSHROOMS

Prep and cook time: 25 min Makes 12 mini quiches

Butter for greasing

Breadcrumbs

2–3 tbsp clarified butter

1 onion, finely chopped

1 garlic clove, finely chopped

225g white mushrooms, chopped

100g oyster mushrooms, chopped

200g cep mushrooms, chopped

350g quark

200g mozzarella cheese, finely chopped

4 eggs

3–4 tbsp semolina or fine oatmeal

50g chopped pine nuts

Salt and freshly ground pepper

Fresh basil, chopped into strips, for garnish

2–3 tbsp pine nuts

Prep and cook time: 1 hour

1 Preheat the oven to 200°C / 400°F / Gas Mark 6. Grease a muffin tin with butter and scatter with bread crumbs.

2 Heat the clarified butter in a pan and sweat the onions and garlic until translucent. Turn up the heat, add the mushrooms and fry for a few minutes.

3 Turn the heat back down, season lightly with salt and pepper and continue frying until all the liquid has evaporated.

4 Beat together the quark, mozzarella, eggs, semolina and pine nuts until smooth and season with salt and pepper.

5 Drain the mushrooms if necessary and add to the quark mixture.

6 Spoon the mixture into the muffin pan and bake in the preheated oven for about 20 minutes until golden brown.

7 Remove from the oven, let cool for 5 minutes then remove carefully from the muffin tin. Serve warm or cold, garnished with basil and pine nuts.

SPINACH QUICHE

Prep and cook time: 40 min plus 30 min chill time

For the pastry:

200g flour

¼ tsp salt

100g butter, cold, chopped, plus extra for greasing

1 egg

For the filling:

2 tbsp butter

1 leek, finely chopped

2 garlic cloves, finely chopped

400g cream cheese

3 eggs

250 ml whipping cream

100g freshly grated hard cheese

450g young spinach, rinsed and roughly chopped

Nutmeg

Salt and freshly ground pepper

1 Preheat the oven to 200°C / 400°F / Gas Mark 6.

2 Pour the flour onto a work surface in a heap and add the salt. Make a well in the middle and scatter with the butter.

3 Crack the egg into the well, add 2–3 tablespoons of lukewarm water and cut all ingredients together with a knife to form a crumbly consistency.

4 Using your hands, knead quickly to a dough, form into a ball, wrap in cling film and chill for around 30 minutes.

5 To make the filling, melt the butter in a pan and gently fry the leek and garlic until soft.

6 Mix the cream cheese with the eggs, cream and half the hard cheese to a smooth consistency.

7 Add the spinach, garlic and leek and season with salt, pepper and nutmeg.

8 Roll the pastry out between two sheets of cling film and use to line a greased 26-cm quiche dish.

9 Pour the filling into the pastry case and smooth the surface. Sprinkle with the remaining hard cheese and bake for around 40 minutes until golden brown.

SALMON WITH HERBS AND LEMON

Prep and cook time: 25 min   Serves 6–8

1 whole salmon fillet, with skin
Salt, to taste

1 lemon

50 ml olive oil

1 small onion, finely chopped

½ bunch parsley, finely chopped

½ bunch basil, finely chopped

⅓ bunch dill, finely chopped

1-cm piece fresh ginger root, peeled and minced

1–2 cloves garlic, minced

Freshly ground pepper, to taste

1 tsp sea salt

1   Preheat the oven to 200°C / 400°F / Gas Mark 6. Grease a long, shallow baking dish (large enough to hold the salmon in a single layer).

2   Lightly salt the salmon. Using a zester or vegetable peeler, zest the lemon and slice into thin slivers. Halve, then juice the lemon into a medium bowl. Add the oil, onion, parsley, basil, dill, ginger, garlic, lemon zest, and pepper.

3   Place the salmon in the baking dish and cover with the lemon-herb mixture. Season with the sea salt. Bake for about 15 minutes or until firm. Serve immediately.

SEASON'S GREETINGS

ROAST TURKEY WITH NUT AND APPLE STUFFING

Prep and cook time: 3 hrs 30 min   Serves 4–6

1 oven-ready turkey, about 2½ kg

2 tsp each of salt, pepper, sweet paprika

2 cooking apples, peeled, cored and diced

Juice of 1 lemon

200g hazelnuts, chopped

100g ground almonds

2 tsp ground cinnamon

75g butter

Salt and freshly ground pepper

For the gravy:

125 ml white wine

300 ml chicken stock

200 ml cream

1 Heat the oven to 200°C /400°F / Gas Mark 6.

2 Rub the salt, pepper and paprika into the cavity of the turkey.

3 Mix together the diced apples and the lemon juice then stir in the hazelnuts, almonds and cinnamon. Stuff the mixture into the cavity of the turkey and sew the opening together with strong thread.

4 Rub the outside of the turkey with the butter, season with salt and pepper and place in a deep roasting pan.

5 Roast the turkey in the oven for 1 hour then baste with the juices and return to the oven for about 1½ hours, basting every 30 minutes. When the juices from the thickest part of the turkey legs run clear remove the turkey from the pan, set aside and keep warm. It should rest for at least 20 minutes before serving.

6 To make the gravy, heat the juices in the roasting pan. Add the wine and the chicken stock, boil for 5 minutes then stir in the cream. Allow to bubble, season with salt and pepper and serve hot.

CHESTNUT STUFFING

Prep and cook time: 25 min

60g fresh chestnuts, peeled, or dried chestnuts soaked overnight

30g fresh breadcrumbs

½ tsp mixed herbs

Salt and freshly ground black pepper

1–2 sticks celery, finely chopped

1 small egg

1 tsp chopped nuts (optional)

1 Put the chestnuts in a pan of water and bring to the boil. Cook until tender – if using dried chestnuts that have been soaked overnight you can omit this step.

2 Drain the chestnuts, reserving some of the cooking liquid to moisten the stuffing if necessary. Mash the chestnuts, then add all the other ingredients and mix well. Add a little of the cooking liquid if the mixture is too dry to hold together well.

3 Use the stuffing in the front end of the bird by loosening the skin away from the body above the neck and pushing in the stuffing. Secure the end of the flap of skin underneath the bird with a cocktail stick, then roast as usual.

APRICOT AND ALMOND STUFFING

Prep and cook time: 10 min plus 3 hours soaking time

25g dried apricots

20g butter

1 small onion, finely chopped

1 small egg

25g flaked almonds, finely chopped

50g fresh breadcrumbs

½ tsp thyme

1 tbsp clear honey

1 Cut the apricots into pieces and place in a bowl of cold water to soak for at least three hours or overnight. Strain and then chop finely.

2 Melt the butter in a frying pan over a medium heat. Add the onion and sauté until soft. Meanwhile, beat the egg.

3 Mix the onion and butter with the apricots, almonds, breadcrumbs, thyme and honey. Add about half the beaten egg and mix into a stiff paste. Add more egg if necessary.

4 Use the stuffing in the front end of the bird by loosening the skin away from the body above the neck and pushing in the stuffing. Secure the end of the flap of skin underneath the bird with a cocktail stick, then roast as usual.

ROAST POTATOES

Prep and cook time: 50 min   Serves 4

800g potatoes, peeled and halved

125 ml sunflower oil

Salt and freshly ground pepper

1 Preheat the oven to 220°C / 425°F / Gas Mark 7.

2 Put the potatoes in a large pan of salted water and bring to a boil. Boil for 5 minutes then drain well. Return the potatoes to the pan and shake hard with the lid on to roughen the surface of the potatoes.

3 While the potatoes are boiling, put the oil into an ovenproof dish and heat in the oven.

4 Carefully add the drained and shaken potatoes to the hot oil and season with salt and pepper. Return the dish to the oven.

5 Roast for 35 minutes, turning once, or until the potatoes are golden brown.

BREAD SAUCE

Prep and cook time: 40 min

1 onion

2 cloves

400 ml milk

1 fresh bay leaf

100g white bread, crusts removed

2 tbsp butter

2 tbsp crème frâiche

Salt and freshly ground pepper

Nutmeg

2 fresh bay leaves, for garnishing

1   Peel the onion and stud it with the cloves.

2   Put the onion, milk and bay leaf in a saucepan and bring to a boil. Simmer very gently for approximately 15 minutes.

3   Remove the onion and the bay leaf.

4   Crumble the bread into the milk. Remove from the heat and allow to soak for 15 minutes.

5   Stir in the butter and crème frâiche. Add salt, pepper and nutmeg to taste.

6   Fill a bowl with the sauce. Serve sprinkled with nutmeg and garnished with the bay leaves.

CRANBERRY AND PISTACHIO SAUCE

Prep and cook time: 40 min

2 onions

300g cranberries

2 tbsp vegetable oil

200g canned tomatoes, chopped

150 ml red wine

100g pistachio nuts

Brown sugar

Salt

Cayenne pepper

1   Peel and coarsely chop the onions.

2   Rinse and drain the cranberries.

3   Sauté the onions in a little hot oil.

4   Mix the cranberries and tomatoes in a pan and pour in the red wine. Coarsely chop the pistachios and add them to the mixture.

5   Simmer the sauce, stirring occasionally, for about 30 minutes.

6   Season to taste with the sugar, salt and cayenne pepper.

ROLLED PORK ROAST WITH HERBS AND PINE NUTS

Prep and cook time: 3 hours   Serves 4

3 tbsp olive oil plus extra for rubbing

1 onion, chopped

3 garlic cloves, chopped

2 red chillies, deseeded and finely chopped

150g pine nuts

50g fresh breadcrumbs

20g thyme leaves

Salt and freshly ground pepper

1 egg, beaten

1 piece pork belly, about 1.2 kg, skin removed

1   Heat the oven to 200°C / 400°F / Gas Mark 6.

2   Heat the oil in a frying pan and gently fry the onion until soft. Add the garlic and the chillies and cook for 2 more minutes. Stir in half the pine nuts, remove from the heat and transfer to a large bowl.

3   Stir in the breadcrumbs and half the thyme leaves and season with salt and pepper. Mix in the beaten egg.

4   Lay the pork flesh side up on a board and place the stuffing along its length. Roll up and secure with kitchen twine.

5   Score the meat with a sharp knife and rub with a little oil, salt and pepper. Transfer the meat to a roasting pan, cover with kitchen foil and roast for 30 minutes.

6   Turn the oven down to 180°C / 350°F/ Gas Mark 4 and roast for a further 1½ hours, basting every 20 minutes.

7   Remove the foil, turn the oven up to 220°C / 425°F / Gas Mark 7, scatter the meat with the remaining pine nuts and thyme and return to the oven for 30 minutes.

8   Let the meat rest in a warm place for 15 minutes before serving.

ROAST HAM WITH PISTACHIOS

Prep and cook time: 1 hour 40 min   Serves 4

1 boned ham joint, about 1 kg, with skin

1 onion, roughly chopped

1 carrot, roughly chopped

2 bay leaves

3 tbsp vegetable oil

4 tbsp honey

2 tsp paprika

Salt and freshly ground pepper

500g pistachio nuts

Fresh herbs, to garnish

1   Put the ham joint in a large pan of water and bring to a boil. Pour the water away, refill the pan with fresh water and put in the onion, carrot and bay leaves. Bring to a boil and simmer for 40 minutes.

2   Heat the oven to 200°C / 400°F / Gas Mark 6.

3   Remove the cooked ham from the pan, cut away and discard the skin and fat and pat the meat dry with kitchen paper.

4   Heat the oil with the honey and paprika in a small pan, season with salt and pepper and brush all over the meat.

5   Chop half the pistachios very finely until they resemble breadcrumbs. Chop the other half very coarsely.

6   Brush the ham with the oil and honey mixture once more then sprinkle the finely chopped pistachios over, pressing so they stick to the meat.

7   Put the meat in a roasting pan, sprinkle over the coarsely chopped pistachios and roast in the oven for 20 minutes. Serve garnished with fresh herbs.

ROAST PARTRIDGE WITH PEARS AND POMEGRANATE SEEDS

Prep and cook time: 1 hour   Serves 4

4 oven-ready partridges

4 tbsp olive oil

Salt and freshly ground pepper

300 ml white wine

150 ml honey

2 onions, peeled and sliced into thick slices

4 pears, peeled

150g pomegranate seeds

1   Heat the oven to 200°C / 400°F / Gas Mark 6.

2   Rub the partridges inside and out with the oil, season with salt and pepper and place in a roasting pan. Roast in the oven for 20 minutes.

3   Heat the wine and honey in a small pan. Remove the partridges from the oven and add the wine/honey mixture to the pan.

4   Add the onions and pears, baste them and the partridges with the pan juices and return to the oven for 20 minutes, basting once more during cooking.

5   Leave the partridges to rest for 10 minutes then serve with the pomegranate seeds sprinkled over.

ROLLED VENISON

Prep and cook time: 2 h 30 min   Serves 6

1.2 kg venison haunch, boned and rolled

Salt and freshly ground pepper

50g butter

1 tbsp black peppercorns, lightly crushed

1 tbsp juniper berries, lightly crushed

12 slices bacon

1 onion, peeled and roughly chopped

1 carrot, peeled and roughly chopped

1 small celeriac, peeled and roughly chopped

1 leek, sliced

125 ml red wine

500 ml game stock

Pinch of sugar

1   Heat the oven to 180°C / 350°F / Gas Mark 4.

2   Season the venison with salt and pepper. Heat 2 tablespoons of the butter in a large frying pan and brown the meat on all sides. Remove the meat from the pan and press the crushed peppercorns and juniper berries into the surface. Wrap the meat in the bacon slices and secure with kitchen twine.

3   Heat the remaining butter in a large ovenproof dish and gently cook the vegetables until soft but not brown. Add the meat then pour over the red wine, let it bubble then add the stock and sugar. Season with salt and pepper then cover the dish and place in the oven for 1½–2 hours or until the venison is tender.

4   When the venison is cooked, remove the dish from the oven and set it aside to rest for 15–20 minutes.

Duck cooked with fruit sauces or other sweet and spicy ingredients creates an exotic meal

DUCK WITH ORANGE

Prep and cook time: 1 hour 50 min   Serves 4

1 oven-ready duck, about 1½ kg

4 oranges, scrubbed and cut into wedges

2 sprigs thyme

4 tbsp red wine

200 ml chicken stock

Salt and freshly ground pepper

1   Heat the oven to 220°C / 425°F / Gas Mark 7.

2   Prick the duck skin all over with a sharp needle to allow the fat to run out. Remove any large clumps of fat from the cavity of the duck and rub the cavity and skin with salt and pepper.

3   Put the wedges from 1 orange into the cavity with the thyme sprigs and put the duck in a roasting pan.

4   Roast in the oven for 20 minutes then carefully drain off the excess fat. Turn the oven down to 180°C / 350°F / Gas Mark 4 and roast for another 30 minutes.

5   Drain off the fat once again, but retain the meat juices. Baste the duck and tuck the remaining orange wedges around it. Return to the oven for another 30–40 minutes or until the juices from the thickest part of the duck legs run clear.

6   Remove the duck and orange wedges from the pan and keep warm.

7   To make the gravy, drain off the fat from the meat juices and heat the juices. Add the the wine to the meat juices, let bubble then add the stock. Simmer for 5 minutes and season with salt and pepper.

Something Special

ROAST BEEF AND YORKSHIRE PUDDING

Prep and cook time: 1 hour 40 min   Serves 4

For the Yorkshire puddings:

1 egg

125 ml milk

2 tbsp water

75g plain flour

Salt and pepper

2 tbsp vegetable oil

For the beef:

1 piece beef fillet, about 1 kg

125 ml vegetable oil

1 tbsp chopped rosemary

1 tbsp chopped thyme

1   Heat the oven to 220°C / 425°F / Gas Mark 7.

2   First, make the Yorkshire pudding batter. Beat the egg, milk and water into the flour to make a smooth batter, season with salt and pepper and set aside.

3   For the beef, rub a little oil over the meat and season with salt and pepper. Heat 100 ml of the oil in a roasting pan and sear the meat until browned all over.

4   Mix the remaining oil with the rosemary and thyme and spread over the top of the meat. Put to roast in the oven.

5   After 10 minutes move the meat down to the middle or bottom shelf and turn the heat down to 200°C / 400°F / Gas Mark 6.

6   After the meat has been cooking for 45 minutes in total, check to see if it is cooked to your liking. Remove from the roasting pan and keep warm.

7   To finish the Yorkshire puddings, grease the holes of a bun tin with the oil and place on the top shelf in the oven for 5 minutes. Pour the batter into the holes of the tin and return to the oven for about 15 minutes or until the puddings are risen and golden brown. Serve the beef and Yorkshire puddings with roasted parsnips and potatoes.

NUT ROAST
WITH CRANBERRIES, SPINACH AND GOAT'S CHEESE

Prep and cook time: 1 hour 20 min Serves 4

150g cashew nuts

150g hazelnuts

125g chestnuts, ready cooked and peeled

3 tbsp sunflower oil

2 onions, finely chopped

2 stalks celery, finely chopped

2 garlic cloves, finely chopped

100g fresh breadcrumbs

100g cranberries

20 sage leaves, chopped

2 sprigs thyme, chopped

4 sprigs parsley, chopped

Salt and freshly ground pepper

Juice of 1 lemon

2 eggs, beaten

200g spinach

200g goat's cheese

1 Heat the oven to 180°C / 350°F/ Gas Mark 4.

2 Sprinkle the cashew nuts, hazelnuts and chestnuts into a dry frying pan and toast over a moderate heat until the nuts are lightly browned.

3 Put the toasted nuts into a food processor and pulse to coarsely chop them.

4 Heat the oil in the frying pan and gently cook the onion and celery until soft. Add the garlic, cook for 2 more minutes then stir in the breadcrumbs and remove the pan from the heat.

5 Put the onion mixture into a large bowl and add the nuts, cranberries and herbs. Season with salt and pepper and stir in the lemon juice and the eggs.

6 Cook the spinach until wilted then drain and squeeze out any excess liquid.

7 Grease a 450g loaf tin and spoon in half the nut mixture, pressing it down with the back of a spoon. Place the spinach on top of the nut mixture in the tin in a neat layer. Spread or slice the goat's cheese over the spinach then add the rest of the nut mixture.

8 Pack the mixture down firmly then bake for 30–40 minutes. Let the loaf cool a little before turning out.

CHRISTMAS PUDDING

Prep and cook time: 6 hours 30 mins plus 4 hours standing time   Serves 6–8

110g raisins

50g currants

110g chopped prunes

175g sultanas

55g candied orange peel, roughly chopped

25 g crystallised or stem ginger, chopped

1 small lemon, finely grated zest and juice

110g molasses sugar

55g chopped almonds

110g breadcrumbs, wholemeal or white

55 g plain flour

1 tsp ground mixed spice

1 tsp ground cinnamon

½ tsp grated nutmeg

½ tsp ground ginger

¼ tsp ground cloves

1 pinch ground allspice

2 large eggs

110g butter, melted

5 tbsp rum or brandy

3 tbsp ginger wine

2 tbsp marmalade, Seville or ginger

Icing sugar, to decorate

1   Combine the dried fruits, peel, ginger, lemon zest, molasses sugar, almonds, breadcrumbs, flour and spices in a mixing bowl.

2   Whisk together the lemon juice, eggs, melted butter, rum and ginger wine. Pour into the ingredients in the mixing bowl and stir in the marmalade. Stir until well combined.

3   Cover with cling film and leave to stand for at least 4 hours or overnight.

4   Butter a 1.2 litre pudding bowl.

5   Spoon the mixture into pudding bowl. Cover with a double layer of pleated buttered greaseproof paper, then with a double thickness of pleated foil.

6   Tie securely and place in a steamer or on an upturned plate in a large pan and pour in boiling water to come halfway up the bowl.

7   Cover the pan and steam for 6 hours, topping up with boiling water as needed.

8   Turn out onto a serving plate and decorate with a sprig of holly and dust lightly with icing sugar.

To make ahead: Cool completely, then wrap in fresh greaseproof paper and foil. Store in a cool, dark place until needed. The pudding will keep for 3 months.

To reheat: steam the pudding for 2 hours.

MINCE PIES

Prep and cook time: 45 min plus 30 min chilling time   Makes 12–15 pies

375g plain flour

250g butter

125g caster sugar, plus extra for sprinkling

1 unwaxed orange, finely grated zest

1 egg, beaten

Orange juice

1 jar (410g) mincemeat

1   Sift the flour into a mixing bowl and rub in the butter until the mixture resembles breadcrumbs. Stir in the sugar and orange zest.

2   Add the egg and just enough orange juice to form a soft but firm dough. Wrap in cling film and chill for 30 minutes.

3   Heat the oven to 190°C / 375°F / Gas Mark 5. Grease 12–15 bun tins or foil cups.

4   Roll out $^2/_3$ of the pastry on a floured surface. Cut into rounds with a 7-cm cutter.

5   Line the tins with the pastry and place a heaped teaspoon of mincemeat in the centre of each.

6   Roll out the remaining pastry and cut out rounds, slightly smaller than the bases. Place on top of the filling and seal the edges.

7   Roll out the pastry trimmings and cut out small stars with a cutter or card stencil. Brush lightly with water and place on top of the pies.

8   Cut a small slit in the top of each pie to allow the steam to escape. Brush the tops with a little water and sprinkle lightly with caster sugar.

9   Bake for 20–25 minutes until lightly golden. Sprinkle with caster sugar and cool in the tins for 10 minutes. Place on a wire rack to cool completely.

CHRISTMAS CUPCAKES

Prep and cook time: 35 min   Makes 12

20g butter

2 eggs

120g caster sugar

3 tbsp whipping cream

115g mincemeat

120g self-raising flour

½ tsp baking powder

1 tsp ground cinnamon

½ tsp freshly grated nutmeg

2 tsp sherry

For the decoration:

120g white marzipan

Red and green food colourings

Icing sugar for dusting

1   Preheat the oven to 180°C / 350°F / Gas Mark 4. Line a 12-hole muffin tin with paper cases.

2   Melt the butter. Mix the eggs and sugar together and beat in the cream. Gently stir in the mincemeat.

3   Sift in the flour, baking powder, cinnamon and nutmeg and fold in until incorporated.

4   Stir in the sherry and melted butter until well mixed. Spoon the mixture equally into the paper cases.

5   Bake in the oven for 12–15 minutes until risen and springy to the touch. Transfer to a wire rack and leave to cool.

6   Divide the marzipan in half. Knead a few drops of red colouring into one half and of green into the other half.

7   Roll out the marzipan on a surface lightly dusted with icing sugar. Cut out festive shapes, such as stars and bells, with small cookie cutters.

8   Place the marzipan decorations on top of each cupcake and sift over a thick layer of icing sugar to decorate.

Festive Fancies

GINGER COOKIES

Prep and cook time: 25 min   Makes 30

150g plain flour

½ tsp bicarbonate of soda

1 tsp ground ginger

1 pinch ground cinnamon

1 pinch ground cloves

55g butter

110g caster sugar

1 small egg, beaten

2 tbsp black treacle

½ tsp lemon juice

75g coarse sugar crystals

1   Heat the oven to 170°C / 325°F / Gas Mark 3. Line 2 large baking trays with non-stick greaseproof paper.

2   Sift the flour, bicarbonate of soda and spices together into a bowl. Set aside.

3   Beat the butter and caster sugar in a mixing bowl until soft and creamy. Beat in the egg.

4   Stir in the treacle and lemon juice, then stir in the flour mixture to form a soft dough.

5   Roll the dough into 2cm balls and roll in the sugar crystals to coat. Place well apart on the baking trays.

6   Bake for about 12 minutes until firm and golden. Cool on the baking trays for a few minutes, then place on a wire rack to cool completely.

SHORTBREAD STARS

Prep and cook time: 40 min   Makes 15–20

For the cookies:

75g unsalted butter, plus extra for greasing baking tray

40g caster sugar

75g plain flour

40g rice flour

1 pinch salt

To decorate:

100g icing sugar

1–2 tbsp lemon juice

1   Heat the oven to 150°C / 300°F / Gas Mark 2. Grease a large baking tray.

2   Beat the butter and sugar until soft and creamy.

3   Sift in the flour, rice flour and salt and mix with your hands to a smooth dough.

4   Roll out on a lightly floured surface and cut into star shapes using a small star-shaped cookie cutter.

5   Bake for 15–20 minutes until pale golden. Cool on the baking tray for a few minutes, then place on a wire rack to cool completely.

6   To decorate, sift the icing sugar into a bowl and gradually beat in enough lemon juice to form a thick coating consistency.

7   Spread the icing over the stars and leave to set.

CHRISTMAS COOKIES

Prep and cook time: 45 min plus 30 min chilling time   Makes 25

130g butter

110g caster sugar

¼ tsp vanilla extract

1 large egg

2 tbsp cornflour

3 tbsp self-raising flour

150g plain flour

110g jam

1 Heat the oven to 190°C / 375°F / Gas Mark 5. Line 2 baking trays with non-stick greaseproof paper.

2 Beat the butter and sugar in a mixing bowl until soft and light. Beat in the vanilla and egg.

3 Sift in the cornflour and both flours and stir until combined. Chill for 30 minutes.

4 Roll heaped teaspoons of the mixture into balls and place on the baking trays. Make a deep indentation in the centre of each ball with a wooden spoon handle dipped in flour.

5 Fill each indentation with ½ teaspoon of jam.

6 Bake for about 20 minutes, until pale golden. Cool on the baking trays for a few minutes, then place on a wire rack to cool completely.

DUNDEE CAKE

Prep and cook time: 2 hours 30 min

180g sultanas

125g finely chopped figs

180g currants

Grated zest of 1 lemon

3 tbsp whisky

6–8 candied cherries, quartered

50g candied lemon peel, finely chopped

50g candied orange peel, finely chopped

250g plain flour

1½ tsp baking powder

180g butter

125g sugar

1 tbsp honey

3 large eggs

75 ml milk

Blanched almonds, for decorating

Icing sugar for dusting

Marzipan (optional), for covering

1 Preheat the oven to 180°C / 350°F / Gas Mark 4. Grease and line a 26cm spring-release cake tin.

2 Mix the sultanas, figs and currants with the lemon zest, whisky and candied fruits in a large bowl and leave to stand.

3 Meanwhile, sift the flour and baking powder together. Cream the butter with the sugar and honey until light and fluffy. Gradually beat in the eggs and then beat in the flour, milk and soaked dried fruit. Turn the batter into the prepared cake tin and smooth the top. Decorate the top of the cake with the whole almonds.

4 Bake in the oven for 30 minutes, then reduce the oven temperature to 150°C / 300°F / Gas Mark 2 and bake for a further 90 minutes. Cover the top with greaseproof paper if it browns too quickly. Cool in the tin for 15 minutes then take out and leave to cool completely.

5 Before serving, dust with icing sugar and cover the sides of the cake with marzipan if desired.

COCONUT CHOCOLATE CAKE

Prep and cook time: 1 hour 30 min

6 eggs, separated
180g sugar
100g plain flour
1½ tsp baking powder
100g grated coconut

For the filling:
50g grated coconut
1½ tbsp cornflour
2 tbsp cocoa powder
225 ml milk
½ tsp vanilla essence
1 tbsp sugar
100g chocolate spread

For the decoration:
200g apricot jam
100g grated coconut
Chocolate curls
Redcurrants

1 Preheat the oven to 180°C / 350°F / Gas Mark 4. Grease a 26cm spring-release cake tin and line with greaseproof paper.

2 Whisk the egg whites with the sugar until stiff. Stir in the egg yolks. Sift in the flour and baking powder and fold into the mixture with the grated coconut. Turn the batter into the prepared cake pan and smooth the top.

3 Bake in the oven for about 40 minutes. Leave to cool slightly, and then remove from the cake pan and leave cool completely.

4 Meanwhile, make the filling. Briefly toast the grated coconut in a non-stick frying pan until lightly browned. Mix the cornflour and cocoa powder with a little of the milk. Pour the remaining milk into a saucepan and gently heat. Add the cornflour mixture, vanilla essence and sugar and bring to the boil, stirring all the time. Add the chocolate spread and sprinkle the surface with the toasted coconut. Leave to cool.

5 To decorate, split the cake horizontally and put the bottom half on a serving plate. Stir the filling mixture and spread on top of the cake half. Place the other half of the cake on top.

6 Warm the apricot jam and spread all over the surface of the cake. Sprinkle the cake on all sides with grated coconut and decorate with chocolate curls and redcurrants.

DARK GANACHE CHOCOLATES

Prep and cook time: 25 min plus 2hours chilling and setting time   Makes 40

250g plain chocolate, 70% cocoa solids

200g milk chocolate, 30% cocoa solids

200 ml double cream

100g butter

2 tbsp instant espresso powder

For the coating:

200g milk chocolate, 30% cocoa solids

150g plain chocolate, 70% cocoa solids

To decorate:

80g icing sugar

2 tbsp double cream

1 Put the cream into a pan and bring to a boil. Break in the chocolate and let it melt in the cream. Stir in the butter and espresso powder. Allow to cool slightly, then chill for at least 1 hour.

2 Using a teaspoon, scoop 40 portions and form into balls. Chill, while you prepare the coating.

3 For the coating: melt the chocolate in a heatproof bowl over a pan of simmering (not boiling) water. Set aside and cool slightly, stirring.

4 Put the chocolates into the melted chocolate, one at a time, and lift out again with a skewer or chocolate fork. Drain and put on non-stick baking paper to set.

5 For the decoration: mix the cream with the icing sugar to make a thick frosting and put into a small piping bag. Pipe a swirl on each chocolate and leave to set.

CHOCOLATE FRUIT AND NUT BAR

Prep and cook time: 30 min plus at least 3 hours chilling time

150g plain chocolate, 70% cocoa solids

350g gianduja, (a blend of chocolate, very finely ground hazelnuts and sugar)

1 tbsp hot espresso

50g chopped blanched almonds

150g candied fruit, (e. g. melon and apricots); chopped

For the coating:

200g chopped plain chocolate, 70% cocoa solids

1 Line a square 15×15cm dish or cake tin with non-stick baking paper.

2 Break up the chocolate and put into a heatproof bowl with the gianduja. Add the espresso and melt over a pan of simmering (not boiling) water, stirring slowly but frequently.

3 Toast the almonds in a dry frying pan over a medium heat, stirring, until golden brown.

4 Stir the almonds and candied fruit into the chocolate mixture and spread smoothly in the tin. Put in a cool place (not the refrigerator) for about 2 hours, to set completely.

5 For the coating: melt the chocolate in a heatproof bowl over a pan of simmering (not boiling) water.

6 Cut the gianduja mixture into 3cm cubes.

7 Using a skewer, dip the cubes into the melted chocolate, one at a time. Place on non-stick baking paper to set in a cool place (not the refrigerator) for at least 1 hour.

Thank you to Jonnie Léger for all her help in producing this book. Thanks also to Gordon Mills,
Marie Clayton and Richard Betts

Published by Atlantic World in 2012

Atlantic Publishing
38 Copthorne Road
Croxley Green
Hertfordshire
WD3 4AQ

© Atlantic Publishing

Recipes by StockFood © The Food Image Agency except 61(top and bottom) and 78.

Images by StockFood © The Food Image Agency except the following : 1 (top left, bottom right & left), 2, 3 (top
left, bottom right & left), 4, 5 (top right & left and bottom right), 6, 12, 20, 29(top), 40, 45(bottom), 47(top), 48, 50(top),
52(top), 57(top), 60, 61(top & bottom), 62(background image), 67, 76, 87(top) and 88 © Getty Images

ISBN 978-1-909242-03-6

Printed and bound in the UK